SECONDARY EDUCATION

A comprehensive critical survey of the controversies, theories and practices central to secondary education today, this book provides teachers, researchers, parents and policy-makers alike with a vital new reference resource.

Secondary Education: The Key Concepts covers a wide range of important topics and debates, including:

- Assessment
- Citizenship
- Curriculum
- E-learning
- Exclusion
- Learning theories
- Work experience

Fully cross-referenced, with extensive suggestions for further reading and on-line resources, *Secondary Education: The Key Concepts* is the essential guide to theory and practice in the twenty-first-century classroom.

Jerry Wellington is Professor of Education at the University of Sheffield. His previous publications include *Teaching and Learning Secondary Science* (Routledge, 2000), *Getting Published* (Routledge, 2003) and *Educational Research: Contemporary Issues and Practical Approaches* (Continuum, 2000).

YOU MAY ALSO BE INTERESTED IN THE
FOLLOWING ROUTLEDGE STUDENT
REFERENCE TITLES

Primary Education: The Key Concepts
Dennis Hayes

Sport and Physical Education: The Key Concepts
Tim Chandler, Mike Cronin and Wray Vamplew

Fifty Major Thinkers on Education
Joy Palmer

Fifty Modern Thinkers on Education
Joy Palmer

Key Concepts in the Philosophy of Education
John Gingell and Christopher Winch

SECONDARY EDUCATION

The Key Concepts

Jerry Wellington

Routledge
Taylor & Francis Group

LONDON AND NEW YORK

First published 2006
by Routledge
2 Park Square, Milton Park, Abingdon, Oxon, OX14 4RN

Simultaneously published in the USA and Canada
by Routledge
270 Madison Avenue, New York, NY 10016

Routledge is an imprint of the Taylor & Francis Group

© 2006 Jerry Wellington

Typeset in Bembo by Taylor & Francis Books
Printed and bound in Great Britain MPG Books Ltd, Bodmin

British Library Cataloguing in Publication Data
A catalogue record for this book is available from the British Library

Library of Congress Cataloging in Publication Data
A catalog record for this book has been requested

ISBN10: 0-415-34403-4   ISBN13: 978-0-415-34403-6 (hbk)
ISBN10: 0-415-34404-2   ISBN13: 978-0-415-34404-3 (pbk)

T&F informa

Taylor & Francis Group is the Academic Division of T&F Informa plc.

CONTENTS

LIST OF CONCEPTS

Accelerated learning
Action research
Affective domain
Alternative frameworks
Assessment
Authentic labour
Authentic learning
Autism/autistic spectrum
  disorders
Bloom's taxonomy
Brain-based learning
Case study
Citizenship
Classroom assistants
Cognition
Cognitive acceleration
Communities of practice
Computer-assisted learning
Constructivism
Continuing professional
  development
Controversial issues
Core skills
Creativity
Criterion-referenced assessment
Critical pedagogy
Cultural capital
Curriculum

Diagnostic assessment
Differentiation
Discovery learning
Dyslexia
Education for sustainability
E-learning
Emotional intelligence
Equal opportunities
Evidence-based practice
Exclusion
Formative assessment
Gifted and talented
ICT
Inclusion
Informal learning
Intelligence
Internet
Key skills
Learning society
Learning styles
Learning theories
Mastery learning
Meaningful learning
Metacognition
Motivation
Multiple intelligences
Pastoral care and PSHE
Peer tutoring

Post–modernism

Problem-based learning

Reflective practice

Secondary education

Situated cognition and situated
  learning

Specialist schools

Spiral curriculum

Thinking skills

Transfer of learning

Work experience

Zone of proximal development

PREFACE

My aim in this book is to provide an introductory but critical summary of a range of ideas, trends, initiatives, theories, labels and concepts in education. I hope that it will be valuable to a variety of people: parents, new and more experienced teachers, governors, researchers not familiar with concepts from outside their own field, and readers with a general interest in education.

Each entry includes references and possible websites to explore. Please note that the selection of material from the World Wide Web is very much my own short-list of sites that I consider interesting and reasonably well written, in some cases from a trawl of potential hundreds of thousands. Many entries have suggestions for further reading. The use of bold in the text indicates that this is a cross-reference to another key concept.

I will certainly be criticised for including certain terms and omitting others but I had to stop somewhere. So what have I included, and why? I have tried to include concepts that I think are interesting and important, and that may be of lasting significance, but time may prove some of my choices wrong. In each case, I have tried to give a brief history of the idea or initiative, wherever possible, and to offer a short speculation on its future.

What have I left out? I have not included terms, trends and ideas that may be short-lived (though again my judgement might well be proved wrong on this) such as 'City Academies', and school 'effectiveness' (surely we won't still be using the term 'effectiveness' in five years from now?). Ultimately, the choice of concepts to include has been a personal one and I fully expect to receive comments on this.

Each entry is built on the evidence and literature currently available. Several include (briefly) my own views and opinions in places. I have been involved in education for 32 years, in school and then in university life, so I feel I definitely have a view after all this time, and it often strikes me as slightly strange when authors keep their own views completely hidden.

If you have any comments or criticisms, praise or grumbles, please e-mail them to: j.wellington@sheffield.ac.uk

ACKNOWLEDGEMENTS

I would like to thank all my 'critical friends' for their valuable feedback on early drafts of many of the entries in this book, especially Wendy Wellington, Hannah Wellington, Jon Scaife and Jackie Marsh.

SECONDARY EDUCATION

The Key Concepts

ACCELERATED LEARNING

Accelerated learning is the notion that a child's (or an adult's) learning can be speeded up by certain means. The means vary but are by no means uncontroversial. For example, the suggestions for accelerating learning put forward by Smith (1996) are summarised by the acronym NO LIMIT. This represents seven principles. The first initial comes from the word k*N*ow: the learner and teacher should know how the brain works in a learning situation – that the brain has different parts, that the right and left sides of the brain should be active and 'linked' and that visual, auditory and kinaesthetic (VAK) inputs can enhance this (see **multiple intelligences** and **metacognition**). The second principle refers to *O*pen and relaxed learners: learning is said to be more enjoyable and longer lasting when the environment is enjoyable and the learner is confident and comfortable. For example, if music is played during a learning situation, this may help create the right environment for some learners. This assertion can be challenged, however; it can be the case that learning, especially outside the classroom, sometimes takes place under stressful or even traumatic conditions, e.g. at the scene of an accident.

The third initial L is for *l*earning: by setting step-by-step targets, learners are given a challenging but supportive environment – experiencing success in achieving targets will motivate learners. *I*nput, the fourth principle, is based on the idea that a variety of inputs is needed, e.g. VAK as above. Fifth, the idea of *m*ultiple *i*ntelligences leads to the principle that different learners have different intelligences that need to be nurtured and different styles in which they learn. Children may be smart in one area, e.g. 'number smart', and can excel in this, if not in other areas. The sixth principle is to *i*nvest in several strategies that can improve self-esteem and enhance learning – these are represented by another acronym, BASIS, with five elements: belonging, aspiration, safety, identity and success (Smith, 1996; Prashnig, 1998). The final initial in NO LIMIT refers to *t*ry it, test it and review it: the idea of constantly reviewing work within a target-setting system.

All the above principles are said to create a supportive learning environment, with a range of sensory inputs, which can motivate learners, enhance their understanding and improve retention of learning (Smith, 1996).

Some of the principles of accelerated learning are said to be based on theories of the brain and how it works. In brief, the brain is said to have three main parts, each with different functions. The 'reptilian brain', at the base of the skull, controls our basic and instinctive functions such as breathing or 'fight and flight'. The middle or 'limbic' brain is the seat of our emotions and long-term memory: it has been suggested that we remember best when our emotions are involved in learning. Finally, the 'neo-cortex' is the area where higher-order thinking skills and problem solving are said to take place. One of the benefits of this model of the brain is the realisation that all parts of the brain, including the emotions, are involved in learning. **Cognition** (i.e. skills, knowledge and understanding) is intimately connected with emotion. Positive emotions can encourage effective learning. Conversely, the implication is that fear and stress can cause activity in the brain to move towards the 'reptilian' section, thus reducing activity in the neo-cortex area – consequently suppressing or even negating learning. Again, this hypothesis could be challenged because learning can occur in stressful or traumatic situations in everyday life.

Furthermore, the thinking part of the brain (the neo-cortex) is said to be in two hemispheres. The right side is responsible for creativity, images and visualisation, music, rhythm and rhyme, art and design, and gaining the holistic picture. The left-side processing involves words, language, logic, number, writing and reading and analytic activity. It has been said that artistic people are 'right-brained' while mathematicians are 'left-brained', though this has been challenged (OECD, 2002).

If we assume that there is some value in these models of the brain, the practical question arises: what is the classroom teacher to do about them, especially when faced with a class of 30 pupils, each with different learning styles and preferences? On the one hand, the teacher could focus on the learning strengths and preferences of individuals and try to build on or exploit them; on the other, they could try to develop the under-developed learning styles in the hope of increasing each learner's repertoire. This is a difficult choice for the classroom teacher to make. In reality, many teachers opt for a mixture of VAK ingredients in their lessons when planning and conducting them, in the hope of giving something to all learners and learning styles.

There are clearly dangers in relying on the two-sided model of the brain too closely as a basis for learning and teaching, especially if learners become labelled as 'right-sided' or 'left-sided' and this is deemed to be their learning style or learning preference, e.g. holistic imagers in contrast to analytic verbalisers.

Accelerated learning has become something of an industry in the twenty-first century, spawning a host of websites and consultancies.

Certain activities and techniques have been developed, allegedly based on theories of the brain, and promoted at in-service and pre-service teacher training events, e.g., 'brain gym', target setting, VAK input and creating conducive environments using music. However sound or unsound the scientific basis for these activities may be, my own view is that the emphasis on improving or even accelerating learning has had certain beneficial effects, e.g. more varied input by teachers built into their lesson planning; increased self-awareness by learners of the way they learn; realisation by teachers that different learners learn in different ways; and the use of activities and environments that can enhance the learning process for many pupils.

See also: **cognitive acceleration**

References and further reading

Lozanov, G. (1979) 'Accelerated Learning and Individual Potential', *Prospects: Quarterly Review of Education*, 9(4): 414–25.

OECD (2002) 'Understanding the Brain: Towards a New Learning Science', *OECD Social Issues/Migration/Health*, 11: 1–10.

Prashnig, B. (1998) *The Power of Diversity: New Ways of Learning and Teaching*, Stafford: Network Educational Press.

Smith, A. (1996) *Accelerated Learning in the Classroom*, Stafford: Network Educational Press.

——(2000) *Accelerated Learning in Practice*, Stafford: Network Educational Press.

Useful websites

http://www.acceleratedlearning.com/method/what_is.html

http://www.alcenter.com/alindex.html

http://www.ncrel.org/sdrs/areas/issues/students/atrisk/at4lk59.htm. This site includes the quote:

> More has been discovered about how the human brain works in the last 15 years than in all history to date. The Accelerated Learning Method is based on that research. We each have a preferred learning style – a way of learning that suits us best. If you know and use the techniques that match your preferred way of learning, you learn more naturally. Because it is more natural for you, it becomes easier.

http://www.funderstanding.com/accelerated_learning.cfm. The DfES National Key Stage 3 strategy contains a wide range of material on accelerated learning at:

http://www.standards.dfes.gov.uk/keystage3/search/?mode=basic_search& pagenumber=1&d=m-ks3&search_string=accelerated+learning

ACTION RESEARCH

This concept originated when Kurt Lewin (1935, 1936, and many subsequent publications) put the approach forward as a means of researching social issues and problems. He suggested a four-phase, continuous cycle of planning, acting, observing and reflecting, then re-planning and so on. This was later adapted by Kolb (1984) (see Figure 1).

In 1975, Lawrence Stenhouse applied the idea of action research to education with his concept of the 'teacher as researcher'. It is still associated with the idea of teacher researchers or indeed any practitioner reflecting upon and researching their own practice in order to improve it. Elliott later expressed the idea in terms of enabling teachers to 'act more intelligently and skilfully' (1992, p. 69) (see **reflective practice**).

Subsequently, various models of action research have been suggested, for example, several advocates have taken Lewin's cycle and adapted it into an action research spiral, a model adapted by John Elliott in terms of a series of successive cycles. The spiral begins when those involved identify or 'diagnose' a particular problem, situation or issue that needs addressing. Discussion and planning follow and this leads to action or 'intervention', which is then monitored and evaluated. After the first cycle of diagnosing, planning, implementing and evaluating, the team will discuss the next stage of the spiral in the light of what has been learnt in the previous phase.

There is no one agreed definition of 'action research'. Carr and Kemmis described it as follows:

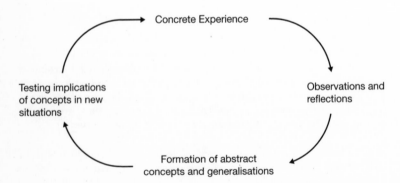

Figure 1 The experiental learning cycle
Source: Developed from the ideas of Kurt Lewin by Kolb (1984)

Action Research is a form of self-reflective enquiry undertaken by participants (teachers, students or principals) in social (including educational) situations in order to improve the rationality and justice of: (a) their own social or educational practices (b) their understanding of these practices and (c) the situations (and institutions) in which these practices are carried out.

(1986, p. 2)

This has often been used as a working definition. Perhaps the key elements of action research are that it aims to do the following:

- to improve practice (as opposed to, say, simply studying it or describing it);
- to raise practitioners' awareness of their own practice;
- to bring about change as its primary aim, rather than just collecting research data and reporting on it;
- to monitor and evaluate any change and then to re-assess and modify the intervention or innovation;
- to be a collaborative effort among people working in the same setting – if 'outsiders' are involved they should work in partnership with insiders;
- to bridge the gap between theory and practice.

Action researchers are more than just external observers (though they may be 'participant observers', a term coined by ethnographers to show the importance in ethnography of observing one's own working environment and questioning its practices and taken-for-granted assumptions).

Action research has been used to focus on many different areas of education including the curriculum, pedagogy (teaching and learning), policy-making, management of educational institutions, and staff development. It is said to have several advantages as compared to 'traditional' approaches to research done by outsiders: the researcher may often be an insider and will know and understand the situation and context of the situation being studied; action research may solve some of the traditional problems associated with the validity of research by allowing triangulation as a result of working collaboratively with others in the situation and reflecting on the process over time; and action research may solve certain ethical problems as it is likely to include those 'being researched' and will show sensitivity towards them. However, it could be argued that other approaches to research can be equally attentive to issues of triangulation and ethics;

and also that action research faces as many problems as it solves, such as the possibility of the researcher being intimately involved in the research situation and therefore being biased or failing to question or 'see' things that an outsider might ('going native' as it is sometimes termed). There can also be ethical difficulties and power issues in researching one's own colleagues or institution.

References and further reading

Carr, W. and Kemmis, S. (1986) *Becoming Critical*, Lewes: Falmer Press.
Elliott, J. (1992) *Action Research for Educational Change*, Buckingham: Open University Press.
Kemmis, S. and McTaggart, R. (1988) *The Action Research Planner*, Geelong, Victoria: Deakin University Press.
Kolb, D. (1984) *Experiential Learning: Experience as the Source of Learning and Development*, Englewood Cliffs, NJ: Prentice-Hall.
Lewin, K. (1935) *A Dynamic Theory of Personality*, New York: McGraw-Hill.
——(1936) *Principles of Topological Psychology*, New York: McGraw-Hill.
McNiff, J. (1997) *Action Research: Principles and Practice*, London: Routledge.

Useful websites

http://actionresearch.altec.org/
http://carbon.cudenver.edu/~mryder/itc/act_res.html
http://www.infed.org/research/b-actres.htm
http://www.infed.org/thinkers/et-lewin.htm

AFFECTIVE DOMAIN

Humans are both thinking and feeling individuals; educators need to consider both, i.e. cognition and affect, as complementary. The affective domain is the component of **Bloom's taxonomy** of educational objectives that involves the feeling and emotional side of learning and teaching, i.e. enjoyment, motivation, drive, passion, enthusiasm, inspiration. Educators have also employed the term 'affect' to describe attitudes, beliefs, tastes, appreciations and preferences.

The affective domain is an important domain for secondary and later phases of education, because it can be ignored by teachers in schools and lecturers in higher education who sometimes assume (wrongly) that all students past the primary phase provide their own motivation and inspiration. It may even explain why some teaching at university level can be so dull and uninspiring. Teachers and lecturers at all levels need to be reminded of this domain.

Why was it forgotten? As behaviourism became more dominant in educational psychology, affect was ruled out by some educators. Humans were viewed through a model of input–process–output with thinking processes which operate like a computer. Often in such a view, affect is seen as 'a regrettable flaw in an otherwise perfect cognitive machine' (Scherer, 1984, p. 293). Now, most researchers who study human behaviour and human nature agree that the views of both extremes – emphasising only affect or only cognition – are undesirable. As Vygotsky put it, the separation of affect from cognition

> is a major weakness of traditional psychology since it makes the thought process appear as an autonomous flow of 'thoughts thinking themselves,' segregated from the fullness of life, from the personal needs and interests, the inclinations and impulses, of the thinker. Such segregated thought must be viewed either as a meaningless epiphenomenon incapable of changing anything in the life or conduct of a person or else as some kind of primeval force exerting an influence on personal life in an inexplicable, mysterious way.
>
> (1962, p. 8)

According to Bloom *et al.* (1956; Kratwohl *et al.*, 1964), the affective domain includes 'objectives' that describe changes in interest, attitudes, emotions and values and the development of appreciation and adjustment. Bloom *et al.* set up a clear hierarchy for the *cognitive* domain, with factual recall at the bottom and understanding near the top. However, in the *affective* domain the hierarchy is less clear but is said to run from awareness and perception of value issues ('receiving' or 'attending') through responding, then valuing, to organising and conceptualising values. The authors clearly found this domain much harder to structure and organise into a neat order. Perhaps it is inappropriate to attempt a hierarchy.

Susan McLeod (see website) suggests that we view the affective domain using two dimensions: intensity and stability. In this view, emotions are intense but unstable (they do not last long); attitudes are less intense than emotions but more stable; and beliefs are less intense and more stable than attitudes. Thus attitudes can be changed, but beliefs are more difficult to change. Motivation would then, in this view, be seen as something involving both affect and cognition.

References and further reading

Bloom, B. S. (ed.) (1956) *Taxonomy of Educational Objectives: The Classification of Educational Goals, Handbook I: Cognitive Domain*, New York: McKay.

Kratwohl, D. R., Bloom, B. S. and Masia, B. (1964) *Taxonomy of Educational Objectives: The Classification of Educational Goals, Handbook II: Affective Domain*, New York: McKay.

Scherer, K. R. (1984) 'On the Nature and Function of Emotion: A Component Process Approach', in Scherer, K. R. and Ekman, P. (eds) *Approaches to Emotion*, Hillsdale, NJ: Erlbaum, pp. 293–317.

Vygotsky, L. (1962) *Thought and Language*, trans. Hanfmann, E. and Vakar, G., Cambridge, MA: MIT Press.

Useful website

http://jac.gsu.edu/jac/11.1/Articles/6.htm (Susan McLeod)

ALTERNATIVE FRAMEWORKS

Every student, of every age, comes into a classroom with some prior learning. This learning may involve skills or information they have acquired, either at home, outside, or in previous classroom experiences. But equally, students will have acquired prior concepts and ideas which have helped them make sense of their experiences. These prior concepts form 'frameworks' through which people understand what they see, read or hear. We all have frameworks by which we make sense of the world, whether we are aware of them or not. We have concepts about the physical/material world and concepts about the 'mental world' (concepts of how our mind and that of other people work). Without these concepts we could not operate successfully in a material or a social world; for example, people who are said to be 'autistic' are sometimes said to have a limited concept of mind, i.e. of how their mind and other human minds work – hence they are said to find it difficult to operate successfully in a social world and to interact with others (see **autism**).

In certain subject areas, such as science, there are accepted concepts and frameworks which are used in that discipline to conceptualise the physical world – or, in the case of psychology, the mental world; for example, physics uses scientifically accepted (at present) ideas of heat, work, energy and power. But many children (and adults) will operate, often successfully, with alternative concepts of, say, heat. For example, many children and adults view heat as a kind of fluid, which 'flows' from a hotter place to a cooler place (and 'cold' flows in the opposite direction). This can be a useful way of thinking about heat (e.g. you shut the window to stop the 'cold' from coming in) but it is not the accepted, established scientific view. Alternative notions or ideas such as these have been labelled 'alternative frameworks'.

In the past, they were sometimes called misconceptions. This is not always helpful for two reasons: first, it assumes that the 'textbook conception', e.g. the scientist's view of heat, is a true one and not subject to change; second, it implies that the alternative conception is not helpful and that people cannot use it to live in the real world. This is patently untrue in the case of heat, where a concept that sees 'heat' and 'cold' as a kind of fluid, flowing from hot areas to cold ones (or vice versa), can be perfectly adequate for many purposes, e.g. stopping draughts in houses.

Why are 'alternative frameworks' important for education and for classroom teachers? First, because students' prior understandings and thoughts about a topic or concept before a lesson exert a tremendous influence on what they learn during teaching and learning. Alternative frameworks have proved remarkably resilient, and are stubborn and difficult to shift. This is true to the extent that students in science, for example, may operate in two 'domains' of thinking – one for the science classroom and the science examination and one for everyday life. Second, because for it to be **meaningful learning**, prior learning and prior conceptions need to be built upon. One of the teacher's primary goals is to bring about a change in the learner's cognitive structure or way of viewing the world. This can best be done by first gaining some knowledge about a student's prior conceptions (see **diagnostic assessment**).

Alternative frameworks are not confined to science learning. They may be present in other school subject areas such as mathematics, geography, history or technology. Equally, outside of school, students can also develop strong alternative frameworks or (mis)conceptions about a wide range of non-scientific areas such as how cars work, how the tax system operates, the process of government, money and money markets, how numbers work and many other areas. And alternative frameworks are not confined to school-age children. Even after several years of schooling, research has shown that people retain 'incorrect ideas' about scientific and other phenomena, e.g. the way that plants or trees grow; or how vision takes place.

Teaching for conceptual change

Learners' alternative frameworks and preconceptions are resistant to change. Learners rely on their own frameworks to understand and get by in their world; they may not wish to discard them and adopt a new way of thinking. Simply 'teaching' a new concept or telling the learners that their views are wrong will not result in conceptual change. One strategy suggested is to create 'cognitive conflict' (see **cognitive acceleration**). This involves creating situations where learners' existing conceptions about particular phenomena or topics are made explicit and then directly challenged in order to create a state of cognitive conflict or 'disequilibrium' (Piaget's term).

Cognitive conflict strategies can be part of Posner *et al.*'s (1982) suggested conditions for bringing about conceptual change. They can be summed up as:

1 There must be dissatisfaction with the currently held conception. If the learner's current understanding and ideas are satisfactory for making sense of a given phenomenon, the learner will be less likely to accept a new conception.
2 The new (to the learner) conception must make sense. Learners must be able to understand what the new conception means.
3 The new conception must appear plausible. Even if the learners understand the newly offered conception, they may not be able to see how it can be applied in a given situation or used to solve a particular problem.
4 The new conception must appear fruitful. It should do more than potentially solve current problems or answer questions. It must be useful in a variety of new situations.

To summarise, learners must become aware of their current conceptions, dissatisfied with them and accept a new notion as *intelligible*, plausible, and *fruitful*.

Teaching for conceptual change is not an easy process; it may often be more time-consuming than traditional, didactic ('tell them like it is') teaching methods. It requires a healthy and supportive classroom environment, where students feel confident talking about and sharing their ideas. Teaching for conceptual change also requires that the teacher should possess good facilitation skills and a thorough understanding of the topic or phenomenon in question.

References and further reading

There is a vast literature on alternative frameworks, but a few key references as starting points are:

Nussbaum, J. and Novick, N. (1982) 'Alternative Frameworks, Conceptual Conflict, and Accommodation: Toward a Principled Teaching Strategy', *Instructional Science*, 11: 183–200.

Posner, G. J., Strike, K. A., Hewson, P. W. and Gertzog, W. A. (1982) 'Accommodation of a Scientific Conception: Toward a Theory of Conceptual Change', *Science Education* 66: 211–27.

Scaife, J. (2000) 'Learning in Science', in Wellington, J. (ed.) *Teaching and Learning Secondary Science*, London: Routledge.

Scott, P., Asoko, H. and Driver, R. (1992) 'Teaching for Conceptual Change: A Review of Strategies', in Duit, R., Goldberg, F. and Niedderer, H. (eds) *Research in Physics Learning: Theoretical Issues and Empirical Studies*, Kiel: Institute for Science Education at the University of Kiel, pp. 310–29.

West, L. and Pines, A. (eds) (1985) *Cognitive Structure and Conceptual Change*, New York: Academic Press.

Useful websites

The following website, 'Constructing history: how historians see the light', illustrates the application of conceptual change to the domain of history (most of the other examples are limited to science topics).
http://www.coe.uga.edu/epltt/cc_example/history1.html
http://www.coe.uga.edu/epltt/ConceptualChange.htm

ASSESSMENT

What is meant by assessment in education? The term is widely debated but rarely defined. The word 'assess' is usually associated with words like measure, gauge, determine, evaluate, judge, weigh up, appraise, and so on. As discussed below, there are many versions and interpretations of assessment. Equally, there is an issue over who or what is being assessed. Is it the student's learning or the teacher's teaching? Is it a course, a curriculum or a method of teaching?

Why should we assess?

The reasons for assessing students vary widely. On a positive note, assessment can serve the following purposes:

- giving feedback to teachers and learners;
- providing motivation and encouragement; acting as both an arm-twister (a stick) and an incentive or reward for some students (a carrot);
- to boost the self-esteem of pupils (equally it can dampen it) and give a sense of achievement;

- as a basis for communication, e.g. to parents, governors or the outside world;
- as a way of evaluating a lesson, a teaching method, a scheme of work or a curriculum;
- to entertain (if done in the right way).

Assessment performs many other functions in society which may not be viewed as positively as the six roles above:

- as a means of ranking pupils so that they can be grouped, streamed or segregated in some way;
- as a means of selection or filtering (sorting and sifting) for either employment or further education;
- to allocate students to a certain choice or pathway, e.g. a career, a new subject choice at the next level up;
- as a way of discriminating or choosing between students for other reasons.

Some different kinds of assessment

The wide range of purposes for assessment can be seen in the types of assessment that can be identified:

1 *Diagnostic assessment* (pre-testing): this is a form of assessment used to evaluate, before and during teaching, every pupil's knowledge, skills and understanding, in order to inform and improve the teaching that is to follow it. The pupils' strengths and weaknesses can be gauged, as can their prior conceptions (see **alternative frameworks**) on the area to be taught and learnt. Diagnostic assessment is essential for a constructivist approach to teaching (see **constructivism**) and forms a good basis for **differentiation**, by enabling teaching to be 'pitched' at the right level and tailored to individuals' needs.

2 *Formative assessment*, also known as assessment for learning: this occurs when assessment is seen as an essential part of the learning process (unlike summative assessment, which takes place after learning is complete). It is another way, like diagnostic assessment, of using assessment to look forward, to guide action and to shape future teaching and learning. Assessment for learning can include self-assessment (in which pupils reflect on and evaluate their own learning) and peer assessment, in which they help to evaluate and think about each other's learning. Formative assessment has

received, quite rightly, increasing attention in recent years (from about 1998 onwards). It has been said to be especially helpful for 'low achievers' and in narrowing the gap between lower and higher achievers (Black and Wiliam, 1998a, 1998b), in contrast to summative assessment, which is said to increase this gap and to demotivate those who don't succeed.

3 *Summative assessment*: this occurs at the end of a teaching unit, a module or a course, such as GCSE or A-levels. Its purpose is usually to give a student a mark, grade or ranking. This form of assessment tends to receive the most publicity in terms of media coverage (school league tables), political debate ('falling standards'), complaints from employers ('we're not supplied with the skills we need') and criticisms from higher education ('A-levels don't discriminate between students at the highest levels'; 'A-levels are too easy').

The importance of variety in methods of assessment

One of the aspects of assessment said to be beneficial is the use by teachers of a wide range of methods and means. Teachers can assess through what they hear and see, as well as what they read. Assessments can be oral or written; they can be formal or informal; they can involve teachers' observations as well as tests; they can consider co-operative group work as well as individual work; they can include coursework as well as tests and examinations. Assessment can involve a variety of outputs: spoken presentations, exhibitions, posters, or portfolios. Assessment can involve the use of ICT: word processing, desktop publishing, PowerPoint presentations, or Internet searches.

Running through all these varied means of presenting and assessing students' work is **Bloom's taxonomy**. This can be used as a checklist so that assessment can be seen to involve not only factual recall but also the use of synthesis and evaluation at the top end of the taxonomy. It should also reflect the affective domain (enthusiasm, motivation, attitude) as strongly as the cognitive (skill, knowledge and understanding).

Current and recurrent debates on assessment

The topic of assessment seems to generate a great deal of debate (hot air in some cases) from educationalists, politicians, universities, employers and parents. Certain issues are current and are certain to recur. Perhaps the main issue for teachers and for parents in the past 20 years has been the huge growth in the sheer volume of assessment. Pupils of all ages seem to have been subjected to an increasing number of formal tests at different stages from 5 to 16. This may have pleased some parents but it has certainly worried others and their offspring. For every single teacher, the rise in the quantity of testing has created a huge demand on their time and energy. The growth era in the volume of assessment saw the popularity of the dubious adage: 'You don't fatten a pig by continually weighing it.'

Another major, recurrent debate has concerned 'standards' and, in most cases, allegedly falling standards. This has occurred as the percentage of pupils obtaining five 'good' GCSEs has risen above 50 per cent and the success rate at Advanced level has grown, with special attention being paid to the numbers gaining three A-levels at A-grade. Some of the 'elite' universities have complained that they need a new means of discriminating between students in the top echelons of A-level; equally, employers have grumbled that standards of literacy and numeracy have fallen despite rising achievement at GCSE and equivalent examinations in Scotland and elsewhere. The standards debate is certain to continue – there can never be an absolute standard in education as there is, for example, for time or for length. The metal rod, exactly one metre in length, housed at a certain temperature in Paris, has no equivalent in education.

A long-standing and complex debate, which I cannot go into fully here, is the question of validity of tests and examinations. What do exams actually measure, apart from a student's ability to do the exam? Can certain qualities, aptitude, potential as an employee or prediction of future success be inferred from examination and test results? The debate is analogous to the old question of **intelligence** testing: what do IQ tests measure other than one's ability to do an IQ test?

Finally, one of the most heated debates in education in the UK and elsewhere has arisen over the publication of examination and test results in the local and national media. Supporters say that this is necessary for parental choice and (even more unfairly) for naming and shaming certain schools. Critics have argued that the examination 'league tables' do little more than reflect the socio-economic class of the students' families. My own view is that any table of results should show the 'added value' developed by the school based on the entry point of the pupils and their 'social capital'.

References and further reading

Black, P. and Wiliam, D. (1998a) 'Assessment and Classroom Learning', *Assessment in Education*, 5(1): 7–71.

——(1998b) *Inside the Black Box: Raising Standards through Classroom Assessment* (occasional paper), London: King's College.

Brooks, V. (2002) *Assessment in Secondary Schools: The New Teacher's Guide*, Buckingham: Open University Press.

Gipps, C. (1995) *Beyond Testing: Towards a Theory of Educational Assessment*, London: Falmer Press.

For discussion of several aspects of assessment in the school context and especially students' self-assessment, see:

McLean, A. (2004) *The Motivated School*, London: Paul Chapman.

Pollard, A. (1997) *Reflective Teaching in the Secondary School*, London: Cassell.

Woodfolk, A. (2004) *Educational Psychology*, Boston: Allyn and Bacon.

Useful websites

http://wiki.literacytent.org/index.php/Assessment_Glossary

http://www.ncrel.org/sdrs/areas/as0cont.htm

On formative assessment:

http://www.fairtest.org/examarts/winter99/k-forma3.html

On diagnostic assessment (sometimes called initial assessment), see:

http://www.dfes.gov.uk/readwriteplus/LearningInfrastructure-DiagnosticAssessment

http://www.keyskillssupport.net/assessment/schoolscolleges/initialAssess.asp

http://www.mmrwsjr.com/assessment.htm

AUTHENTIC LABOUR

A very useful idea in considering whether **computer-assisted learning** (CAL) actually adds value to the learning process – or perhaps detracts from it – is the notion of 'authentic labour'. The issue of authentic labour arises as a direct result of the ability of computers to act as labour-saving devices. Computers used as word processors, to carry out calculations using a spreadsheet, to store data in a database or to collect or 'log' data in a science laboratory are all being used to 'save labour'. But is the labour they save or by-pass an authentic (important) learning experience? Does the use of CAL in saving labour take away an important educational experience for a student? For example, the ability to write by hand, the skill of calculating, the ability to store or hunt for data manually, and the skill of collecting data, taking readings, recording them and starting to process them can all be by-passed by **ICT**. The only strong argument for this by-pass is that the learner can then progress to higher-order skills and skip the mundane, lower-order drudgery of, say, calculating or taking readings. The argument against is that certain authentic learning experiences or skills are thereby ignored and thus wither, atrophy and die, e.g. mental arithmetic or the ability to read a meter, a dial or a thermometer (summarised in Scaife and Wellington, 1993). It can be argued that certain skills and abilities should be part of the aims of education. These aims could include: the ability to search for information in printed books and documents; handwriting; the ability to perform calculations without an aid. Will the increased use of ICT in learning make these aims obsolete? Should this be allowed to happen?

My own view is that the jury is still out on this one and always will be; it will remain a perennially debated question. ICT use in education will always by-pass certain skills and labour; this may be a good thing if higher-order skills and activities are engaged in. But teachers and educators need to be aware of the authentic and inauthentic labour in every context and ensure that abilities do not become atrophied. This question must always be posed: 'Does use of the computer in saving labour take away an important educational experience for the learner?'(discussed fully in Scaife and Wellington, 1993).

See also: **e-learning**, **ICT**, the **Internet**.

References and further reading

Scaife, J. and Wellington, J. (1993) *Information Technology in Science and Technology Education*, Buckingham: Open University Press.
Wellington, J. (1999) 'Integrating Multimedia into Science Teaching: Barriers and Benefits', *School Science Review*, 81(295): 49–54.

AUTHENTIC LEARNING

One of the criticisms levelled at traditional school teaching is that it is disconnected and disembedded from students' experiences outside the classroom. The learning tasks lack meaning for the student. Advocates of 'authentic learning' argue that learning tasks should be embedded in problem-solving contexts that are relevant in the real world. Learners must see the relevance to their lives of the knowledge and skills they learn, and the way these can usefully be applied to problems they see as important. The tasks may be problem-based or case-based. A carefully designed task or problem should create a situation which requires and motivates learners to acquire the knowledge and skills needed in solving the problem (see **problem-based learning**).

Thus, so-called 'authentic classrooms' will anchor learning in real-world cases and issues. Students will decide for themselves the order in which they go about their task. Assessment activities are derived from the task undertaken. Students will often be expected to present the product of their learning to an audience that goes beyond the class and the teacher, e.g. to a local community group.

ICT can often help teachers to incorporate authentic tasks into their lesson (Selinger, 2001). Good software on disc, Internet connections and web resources allow students to take part in simulated, real-world activities and to research and collaborate with real experts. The Internet can be used for gathering information on local or global problems; ICT can be used in presenting the case and reporting back, whatever the audience. Thus authentic tasks are often centred on real-life situations where students require an authentic audience. The authentic task is usually made up of many smaller discrete parts that require the student to problem-solve, to analyse data, and to organise information, and that involve complex thought. Indeed, it is often argued that authentic learning activities provide unique opportunities for students to engage in the higher-level thinking skills in **Bloom's taxonomy**, i.e. analysis, synthesis and evaluation, that are often not reached in classroom activity. It is also said that authentic tasks provide students with a reason or relevancy for learning, i.e. **motivation**.

Authentic pedagogy

Authentic approaches to teaching and learning provide many new opportunities for students and teachers. The teacher's role is changed from that of the sole information giver to that of a facilitator for our students ('sage on the stage to guide on the side', to use the cliché). Ideally, a full community of learners should be incorporated in authentic learning, which could include the teachers, students, local people, parents, and outside experts.

Newmann's (1996) research indicates that 'authentic pedagogy' has a positive effect on student achievement. However, he goes on to say that we should not abandon all forms of 'inauthentic' work in school (we should keep authentic activities as the ideal valued end product) – partly because advocates of authentic learning have found that implementing authentic pedagogy is far from easy. Teachers are said to be so accustomed to the traditional style of pedagogy that a change to authentic style is really challenging for most. Many students also may have difficulty in changing their 'school learning style' from traditional to authentic.

Teachers wishing to implement this pedagogy may also meet resistance from senior management, governors and parents who may be sceptical of something so radically different from the traditional classroom.

Authentic pedagogy is said to have four main elements:

1 knowledge construction;
2 connections of learning to students' personal worlds;
3 learning beyond school;
4 cooperation and communication.

According to Newmann (1996), authentic learning environments have to meet these criteria in order to qualify as an 'authentic learning classroom'. Similarly, Gordon (1998) suggests that authentic learning involves students actively solving problems, working together as a group, using their knowledge, skills, and attitudes, building on what is meaningful to them, connecting activities to previous tasks. There should also be public displays of the learning of the child. He sees the teacher as the designer, coach, and giver of feedback in the process of authentic learning. The teacher designs the task, with specific objectives and goals. The teacher helps students develop their skills and knowledge, shape their strategies, and find resources. The teacher is also the person who creates the structure for assessment. He or she oversees the reflection of the students as they talk about their products, processes and share their understanding of the task. The teacher also works with students on self-reflection.

Conclusion

Authentic learning allows students to explore, discover, discuss, and meaningfully construct concepts and relationships in contexts that involve real-world problems and projects that are relevant and interesting to the learner. Authentic learning implies several things: that learning be centred on authentic tasks; that learning be guided with teacher scaffolding; that students be engaged in exploration and inquiry; that students have opportunities for social discourse; and that ample resources be available to students as they pursue meaningful problems. Advocates of authentic learning believe these elements support natural learning, and many of these ideals are based on theory and research on learning and cognition

References and further reading

Gordon, R. (1998) 'Balancing Real-World Problems with Real-World Results', *Phi Delta Kappa*, 79: 390.

Newmann, F. (1996) *Authentic Achievement: Restructuring Schools for Intellectual Quality*, San Francisco: Jossey-Bass.
Selinger, M. (2001) 'Setting Authentic Tasks Using the Internet', in Leask, M. (ed.) *Issues in Teaching Using ICT*, London: RoutledgeFalmer.

Useful websites

http://crossroads.georgetown.edu/vkp/resources/glossary/authenticlearning.htm
http://tiger.coe.missouri.edu/~vlib/
http://www-personal.umich.edu/~tmarra/authenticity/authen.html

AUTISM/AUTISTIC SPECTRUM DISORDERS

The label 'autism' is still used but it is now more common to refer to the autistic spectrum disorder (ASD). This includes autism ('absorbed in the self': Berk, 2003), high functioning autism, Asperger's Syndrome and Pervasive Developmental Disorder Not Otherwise Specified (PDDNOS or PDD for short).

Estimates vary as to the prevalence of ASD in school-aged children. One estimate available (December 2001) is that approximately 8 people in 1000 (about 0.8 per cent) are affected by some degree of autistic spectrum disorder (further details and discussion of the UK context can be found on the excellent website of the National Autistic Society at www.nas.org.uk). It is estimated that there are 4 males to every female with 'classical autism' and 9 males to 1 female with Asperger's Syndrome.

A long list of challenges posed by ASD includes the following elements, all of which relate to the experience of teachers:

1 Problems in attuning to social situations: pupils may have problems with social interaction, responding to verbal and non-verbal cues and using 'social language'. This may also mean that they do not respond to humour, e.g. use of a pun or other joke, irony, or certainly sarcasm. Pupils may show inappropriate social behaviour, perhaps leading to rejection by peers.
2 Problems with communication. Language is disordered or in extreme cases speech never develops at all and the child is non-verbal. At the other extreme, a person's language may appear normal but the use of language is impaired (Asperger's).
3 Pupils may interpret instructions and explanations literally; this can be a problem when metaphor, analogy or idiom (such as 'horses for courses') is used. This is discussed later.

4 Pupils may have their own personal agendas during a lesson and go off entirely on their own track. The old phrase 'he's got a mind of his own' may have a more poignant meaning than usual in this context. All pupils have their own agendas, but pupils with ASD may have more 'personal agendas' than most, which they may follow in classroom activities or practical work but also when asked to do their own research or to search for information, e.g. on the Internet.

5 Obsessive behaviours: many pupils may become completely engrossed in a certain topic or line of enquiry and this is often to be welcomed. This happens with many topics and 'The Dinosaurs' is probably the classic, but some pupils with ASD may become totally obsessed with one aspect of a subject, e.g. the periodic table in science, certain aspects of mathematics or number work. This obsession may then impede their learning in other areas.

6 Another feature often discussed is the inability of students or adults with ASD to 'read other people's minds' (see Berk, 2003, pp. 442–3). Most people are able to detect mental states, such as disapproval or pleasure, in others by inferring them from things we observe, i.e. cues such as a smile, a frown or a grimace. These inferences are allegedly not made by someone on the ASD, partly perhaps because they do not make the observations (such as eye contact) on which the inference would be based. Consequently, words such as 'feel', 'pretend' and 'believe' are often not part of the vocabulary of ASD children who can speak; and 'make-believe' play is often absent.

The main features of ASD were summed up in the form of a triad by Uta Frith (see Figure 2).

One of the key features of autism, which impinges on learning and teaching, is the pupil's tendency to interpret language (spoken but also written) *literally*. This can be a particular problem in subjects which involve general ideas and abstractions. For example, science teachers depend on the use of analogy in order to explain difficult ideas and abstract concepts. They use the water analogy to convey the idea of a current or a flow – this analogy is sometimes taken further in likening a cell or battery to a pump, which 'pushes' water around the circuit. Resistance has been taught in a similar way, e.g. relating it to the width of a water pipe. This analogy and other analogies and metaphors are widespread in teaching. We talk about a 'sea of air' above us in explaining atmospheric pressure, we use the idea of a field, we talk about light as being a wave and we sometimes attribute human characteristics to non-human objects (anthropomorphism) in order to make scientific ideas more accessible. Some pupils will take these literally. For example, in science teaching for one pupil the digestive system had been likened to a washing machine and as a result he literally thought that food is washed during digestion.

Teachers cannot avoid metaphor in explaining new, unfamiliar ideas – physics, especially, depends on it for explaining abstract concepts. But in teaching via metaphor and analogy *all* teachers need to be extremely vigilant in ensuring that they are taken as such and not interpreted literally – this requires use of phrases like 'we can see X as if it were like … '.

Alleged causes of autism

Research findings appear to vary on the causes of autism, and debate on the 'scientific' research is highly controversial and sometimes emotional. It is said that those on the autistic spectrum have no 'theory of mind', i.e. knowledge of others' mental states and perhaps their own (see **metacognition**). But this is not an explanation of the root causes.

There are now some reports of an alleged connection between autism, epilepsy and behaviour, but again this is not a causal explanation. Some have argued that the cause is innate, i.e. some kind of impairment in the brain that the child is born with. Others have argued, controversially, that autism may be linked to an early event such as the MMR (measles–mumps–rubella) inoculation, which has

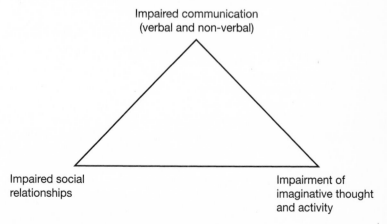

Impaired communication
(verbal and non-verbal)

Impaired social
relationships

Impairment of
imaginative thought
and activity

Figure 2 The triad of impairments associated with autistic spectrum disorders
Source: Frith (2003), triad based on the work of Lorna Wing

been said to have this unwanted side effect in a small proportion of cases (see http://www.cdc.gov/nip/vacsafe/concerns/autism/autism-mmr.htm. and numerous other websites). However, this research has recently been discredited.

References and further reading

Berk, L. (2003) *Child Development*, Boston: Allyn and Bacon.
Fitzpatrick, M. (2004) *MMR and Autism: What Parents Need to Know*, London: Routledge.
Frith, U. (2003) *Autism: Explaining the Enigma*, 2nd edn, Oxford: Basil Blackwell.
Gupta, V. B. (ed.) (2004) *Autistic Spectrum Disorders in Children*, New York: Marcel Dekker/London: Taylor and Francis.
Howlin, P. (1997) *Autism: Preparing for Adulthood*, London: Routledge.

Useful websites

The Key Stage 3 National Strategy website has some useful links to resources on autism at:
http://www.standards.dfes.gov.uk/keystage3/search/?mode = basic_search
   &pagenumber = 1&d = m-ks3&search_string = autism
   If you type the word 'autism' into Google and then search, you will get just under 5 million 'hits'. The addresses below are all useful from a teaching and learning perspective but I am certain there will be many more:
http://www.autism.net/
http://www.autismwebsite.com/
http://www.cdc.gov/ncbddd/dd/ddautism.htm
http://www.naar.org/
http://www.nimh.nih.gov/Publicat/autism.cfm
   TEACCH (Treatment and Education of Autistic and Communication Handicapped Children) is a programme which originated in the USA but is now worldwide. See, for example:
http://www.asatonline.org/about_autism/autism_info14.html
http://www.teacch.com/teacch.htm

BLOOM'S TAXONOMY

This is a taxonomy (a classification) that was developed in the 1950s but experienced a revival at the start of the twenty-first century and has now passed its fiftieth birthday. It was originally written (Bloom, 1956; Kratwohl *et al.*, 1964) as a way of classifying different types of 'educational objectives', but now is often seen as a way of considering different types of learning and putting them into levels (a hierarchy). Bloom is usually given the credit for it but actually a team of five authors (all American males from Chicago) was jointly responsible, with a list of 34 others contributing between 1949 and 1956. Benjamin Bloom was fortunate in having the surname that came first in the alphabet.

The stated aim was to provide a 'classification of the goals of our education system' on which teachers could build a curriculum. It was very much a product of its era, a time when behaviourist psychology ruled the roost (see **learning theories**) and learning objectives had to be specified in terms of what students could actually do as a measurable end product of the learning process. As well as a framework for testing pupils, one use suggested for it was as a tool to analyse a teacher's success in classroom teaching (Bloom, 1956, p. 3). Now it is used as a checklist in lesson planning and classroom questioning (see later).

The principle underpinning the enterprise was 'The view of the group is that educational objectives stated in behavioural form have their counterparts in the behaviour of individuals. Such behaviour can be observed and described and these descriptive statements can be classified' (ibid., p. 5).

The taxonomy was to be divided into three domains: the cognitive, the affective and the psycho-motor. Bloom never completed work on the latter domain, although Dave presented a version of it in 1975.

First, the *cognitive domain*: this is the domain of knowledge and intellectual abilities and skills. It is also said to include the 'behaviours': remembering, reasoning, problem solving, concept formation and creative thinking. The taxonomy in this domain actually became a hierarchy of six major classes, moving from simple to complex (see Figure 3). The objectives in the higher classes were said to build on the 'behaviours' in the preceding classes:

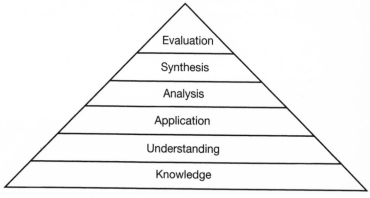

Figure 3 Bloom's taxonomy

1 Knowledge
2 Understanding
3 Application
4 Analysis
5 Synthesis
6 Evaluation

Second, the *affective domain*: this includes 'objectives' that describe changes in interest, attitudes, emotions and values and the development of appreciation and adjustment. In this domain, the hierarchy was spelt out far less clearly but was said to run from: awareness and perception of value issues ('receiving) through responding, then valuing, to organising and conceptualising values.

Finally, the *psycho-motor*: the analysis of this domain was even less well developed by Bloom *et al.*, but ranges from imitation and reflex movements at the lower end to manipulation and then skilled, articulated and precise movements at the upper level.

The main focus of Bloom and the team's work was the cognitive domain. One reason given for this was that the cognitive was said to involve a high level of consciousness and awareness in contrast to the affective, said by Bloom *et al.* to involve 'lower levels' of consciousness and awareness. This would certainly be disputed now with increased emphasis on concepts such as **emotional intelligence**. Anyway, the Bloom team went on to sub-divide the cognitive domain into several subsets:

1.00 Knowledge, which is mainly about remembering and factual recall, was divided into:
1.10 knowledge of specifics;
1.11 knowledge of terminology, e.g. symbols, scientific words, terms used in geometry;
1.12 knowledge of specific facts, e.g. dates, events, places, people;
1.20 knowledge of ways and means of dealing with specifics, e.g. organising, judging, criticising ideas and phenomena;
1.21 knowledge of conventions, e.g. usages, rules;
1.22 knowledge of trends and sequences, e.g. processes, changes over time/evolution, causes and effects;
1.23 knowledge of classifications, e.g. types of material, genres of literature;
1.24 knowledge of criteria for testing or judging, e.g. the nutritional value of a meal, the worth of a work of art;

1.25 knowledge of methodology, e.g. inquiry techniques in a field, 'scientific method' (author's note: highly problematic);

1.30 knowledge of the universals and abstractions in a field, e.g. principles, laws, explanations, theories.

2.00 Comprehension/understanding was divided into:

2.10 translation, e.g. summarising a piece of writing, simplifying a problem in technical language into simpler terms, stating in 'your own words', giving an example or illustration of an abstract idea; reading a plan;

2.20 interpretation, e.g. looking for general ideas, interpreting data, distinguishing warranted from unwarranted conclusions from a body of data or evidence;

2.30 extrapolation, e.g. drawing conclusions, making inferences, predicting trends and consequences.

3.00 Application (not sub-divided). For example, applying abstractions (such as laws, theories, rules or principles) to particular, often practical, situations, i.e. actually using 2.00, understanding, correctly solving problems by using acquired skills and knowledge.

4.00 Analysis: this will involve activities such as seeing patterns, identifying key components, dissecting arguments. It was subdivided into:

4.10 analysis of elements, e.g. recognising unstated assumptions; distinguishing conclusions from their supporting evidence or 'facts from hypotheses';

4.20 analysing relationships, e.g. between interconnecting ideas; distinguishing cause and effect from other types of relationship; detecting logical fallacies in an argument;

4.30 analysis of organisational principles, e.g. form and pattern in literary or artistic work; recognising a writer's bias in an historical account or rhetoric in a persuasive account such as an advertisement or political speech.

5.00 Synthesis: this involves integrating ideas, creating novel ideas from old ones, producing a 'unique communication', connecting and relating knowledge from different areas, producing conclusions and generalisations. This was sub-divided into:

5.10 producing a unique communication, e.g. creative writing of a story or poem, writing a short musical composition;

5.20 production of a plan or a proposed set of operations, e.g. devising a way of testing a hypothesis, planning a lesson or a scheme of work for pupils, designing a simple machine to perform an operation, or designing a building for a certain function;

5.30 derivation of a set of abstract relations, e.g. formulating a hypothesis, making a mathematical discovery (an example cited by Bloom *et al.* as being at the highest level here is the development of the periodic table in chemistry).

6.00 Evaluation: this involves assessing, judging, appraising, weighing up, criticising or defending a hypothesis, theory or argument. It is placed at the top of the hierarchy since it is said to involve all the other 'behaviours' from knowledge upwards. It also provides a link to the affective domain of values and value judgements. Two sub-divisions were described:

6.10 judgements in terms of internal evidence and criteria, e.g. using internal standards;

6.20 judgements using external criteria, e.g. comparing major theories in an area.

The taxonomy in the present day

It is interesting that this 1950s' classification is still used and referred to extensively over 50 years later. For example, it features in the National Key Stage 3 strategy in England and Wales (see the DfES Key Stage 3 Strategy website for details). One specific application is in considering the types and the range of questions that teachers should pose in the classroom in order to stretch pupils and to cater for all 'abilities'. Classroom questioning should include open and closed questions, and questions at different levels of the cognitive hierarchy, i.e. a range running from lower-order questions (asking simply for factual recall) up to the higher order, such as evaluating and criticising. The words, often called 'question cues', that teachers might use at each level are:

- *Knowledge*: Recall, list, define, identify, name, describe. Who, when, what, where?;
- *Understanding*: Translate, summarise, interpret, contrast, predict, discuss. Why?;
- *Application*: Apply, demonstrate how, solve, classify; discover; try in a new context;
- *Analysis*: Explain how, infer (what if?), separate, connect, order, compare and contrast, analyse;
- *Synthesis*: Design, combine, integrate, modify, generalise, create, compose;

- *Evaluation*: Assess, decide, rank, conclude, summarise, compare and contrast, judge.

Bloom's taxonomy can be criticised for its highly behaviourist approach, with its stress on measurable outcomes and specifiable objectives. It is also weak in its lack of stress on 'affect' or the affective domain. One could also question whether the levels do indeed form a linear progression and are cumulative, i.e. can a higher level be reached without the previous levels? But if we ignore some of these potential criticisms, and the behavioural aspect of the original enterprise, it can be seen to have value in considering forms of learning and in specific areas such as lesson planning and classroom interaction, or as a checklist in assessing students' work to see which of the levels in the hierarchy they may have reached.

References and further reading

Bloom, B. S. (ed.) (1956) *Taxonomy of Educational Objectives: The Classification of Educational Goals, Handbook I: Cognitive Domain*, New York: McKay.

Harrow, A. (1972) *Taxonomy of the Psychomotor Domain: A Guide for Developing Behavioural Objectives*, New York: McKay.

Kratwohl, D. R., Bloom, B. S. and Masia, B. (1964) *Taxonomy of Educational Objectives: The Classification of Educational Goals, Handbook II: Affective Domain*, New York: McKay.

Useful websites

http://www.brad.ac.uk/acad/health/internal/sjw/DOMAINS/tsld001.htm

http://www.dmu.ac.uk/~jamesa/learning/bloomtax.htm (Atherton, J. S., 2003, 'Learning and Teaching: Bloom's Taxonomy', [on-line] UK)

http://www.duncanwil.co.uk/bloomcog_files/frame.html

Bloom received something of a revival with the National Key Stage 3 strategy of the DfES. Choose from a range of pages at:

http://www.standards.dfes.gov.uk/keystage3/search/?mode = basic_search &pagenumber = 1&d = m-ks3&search_string = Bloom%27s+taxonomy

BRAIN-BASED LEARNING

The late 1990s and the early twenty-first century saw a huge growth in several related trends that can be grouped under the label of 'brain-based learning' (BBL) (indeed, the 1990s were designated the

'Decade of the Brain' in the USA). These trends, some would say bandwagons, were given labels such as brain gym, personalised learning and whole-brain thinking. The movements are also linked to ideas and initiatives such as **accelerated learning, thinking skills, learning styles** and learning preferences, such as VAK (visual, auditory, kinaesthetic) and **multiple intelligences**.

For example, 'whole-brain thinking' (http://www.bellaonline.com/articles/art28465.asp) is said to occur when the two hemispheres of the brain work together to create a 'whole brain thinking pattern'. This is said to enhance our logical thinking, intuition, analytical skills and artistic ability – quite a tall order. The idea is based on the theory that the two cerebral hemispheres are responsible for different aspects of our thinking/cognition. The 'left brain' is thought to be the location of logical, rational, sequential, analytical, objective and rational thinking; the right brain is the intuitive, aesthetic, holistic, synthesising and subjective part. Allegedly, most learners and thinkers have a definite preference for one side or the other but some people are said to be capable of using both hemispheres and both modes of thinking.

Advocates of whole-brain thinking claim that engineers and scientists are often left-brain thinkers, while most poets and artists are right-brain thinkers, though the evidence for this is somewhat hazy. Some of history's greatest inventors and pioneers, such as Leonardo da Vinci, are said to be whole-brain thinkers.

It is said that schools and formal education tend to emphasise the use of the analytic, logical half and play down the holistic right brain. They do not give enough weight to the creative, imaginative, synthesising right hemisphere. This can be rectified by including more activities such as patterning, role playing, visual activity and the use of metaphors and analogies. This must be matched by new forms of assessment, which value and involve right-brain activities.

Brain gym

Brain gym is said to have originated in the 1970s with the work of educators Paul and Gail Dennison (Dennison and Dennison, 1974) (it is sometimes called educational kinesiology). It is basically a range of simple movements or exercises designed to engage, energise and relax students, and prepare them for learning. Advocates of 'brain gym' argue that its use can get the two halves of the brain working together and that it can bring about clear and rapid improvement in pupils' concentration, memory, reading, writing, organising, listening and physical coordination. Some examples of the actual activities (from a list of almost 30) that pupils are encouraged to do are:

- *head patting and tummy rubbing*: pat your head with your right hand whilst rubbing your tummy with your left; do this 20 times, then swap hands;
- *lazy 8s*: draw the figure 8 three times in the air or on paper with each hand about three times, then with both hands together;
- *writing your name in the air*: first with each hand and then with both hands – again, the bigger the better;
- *double doodle*: draw with both hands at the same time, in, out, up and down;
- *neck rolls*: breathe deeply, relax your shoulders and drop your head forward. Allow your head to slowly roll from side to side as you breathe out any tightness. Your chin draws a smooth curve across your chest as your neck relaxes;
- *belly breathing*: rest your hand on your abdomen. Blow out all the old air in your lungs in short, soft little puffs. Take a slow, deep breath, filling up gently, like a balloon. Feel your hand softly rise as you inhale and fall as you exhale. If you arch your back after inhaling, the air goes even deeper.

Brain gym has become a worldwide movement, some would say an industry, and a brief surf through the World Wide Web will show you a wide range of sites, some more evangelical than others, on this area. Two interesting starting points are:

- http://www.braingym.org.uk/
- http://www.tagteacher.net/grapevine/index.htm?http://www.tagteacher.net/ubb/Forum2/HTML/000372.html

Why have schools seized upon brain-based learning?

It seems that many schools in the late twentieth and early twenty-first centuries latched on to BBL, for understandable reasons. Some were perhaps searching for 'scientific authority' for the way they were working with a huge variety of learners, learning styles and learning preferences. Others were perhaps desperately seeking ways of improving learning and attainment in schools that were said to be 'failing' by inspectors and the media. It could be said, harshly, that they were clutching at straws. Others may have genuinely been persuaded by the science behind BBL and were able to see its benefits in the classroom for pupils, e.g. by introducing variety into lessons; by having actual breaks (such as brain gym) in lessons; or using brain gym activities to get lessons started and pupils focused. For many teachers, it worked and still works and that is justification enough – whatever the neuro-scientists, using the latest scanning techniques, discover or hypothesise about the human brain.

Critics and sceptics

Throughout the history of education, as a movement springs up and gains momentum, so do its critics, rather like predator and prey. For example, Bruer (1997) argued strongly against the claims made by certain brain-based learning advocates: 'these ideas have been around for a decade, are often based on misconceptions and over-generalizations of what we know about the brain, and have little to offer to educators'. He claimed that the advocates of BBL are trying to 'build a bridge too far'.

In a similar vein, Ravitch (2000) called brain-based learning a troubling trend, and a 'distortion of what cognitive scientists have learned about how children learn'. She suggested that brain-based learning might be a commercial bandwagon. My own observations of the proliferating number of courses, companies and consultants offering expensive workshops and resources on BBL support her view of its commercial impact.

One of the most popular BBL texts has been heavily criticised for its style over content approach, for its lack of scientific rigour and for being an ideas book rather than a research-based factual account.

Despite its critics, many educators and researchers continue to follow the theory and practice that come under the broad label of 'brain-based learning'. Some classroom teachers who have taken aspects of it into their practice seem to be firmly convinced that it makes a positive difference to learning and lessons. Many teachers, for example, advocate the classroom use of ideas such as: the provision of drinking water, intermittent physical activity and lesson breaks, giving children an insight into the way the brain works, brain gym, VAK checklists in lesson planning and the sharing of learning objectives with pupils. The question of how effective BBL techniques are in improving learning remains open but there is no doubt that the publicity given to BBL has made an enormous impact on certain teachers. The movement, and the industry behind it, look set to continue.

To end on a positive note: the emphasis on 'brain-based learning' has certainly been one of the important factors contributing to the increased focus on *learning* that is now a welcome feature in educational debate. Certainly, there are four important points about learning that owe some debt to BBL: first, that a multi-sensory approach to learning and classroom teaching is vital – learning and teaching should involve visual aspects (pictures, images, diagrams), auditory activity (listening, speaking, using words) and kinaesthetic activity (touch, movement); second, psychological, emotional and physical safety and security are essential for learning to take place; third, it is vital that learners are active, engaged and in control of their own learning; and finally, research on the brain has shown that it has huge, untapped potential in terms of the billions of neurons and interconnections between them that could be made but are not, even in the most famous of brains, such as Einstein's, which have been studied post-mortem.

References and further reading

Bruer, J. T. (1993) *Schools for Thought: A Science of Learning in the Classroom*, Cambridge, MA: MIT Press.

——(1997) 'Education and the Brain: A Bridge Too Far', *Educational Researcher*, 26(8): 4–16.

Caine, G., Nummela-Caine, R. and Crowell, S. (1999) *Mindshifts: A Brain-Based Process for Restructuring Schools and Renewing Education*, 2nd edn, Tucson, AZ: Zephyr Press.

Campbell, L. (2002) *Mindful Learning: 101 Proven Strategies for Student and Teacher Success*, Thousand Oaks, CA: Corwin Press Inc.

Dennison, P. and Dennison, G. (1974) *Brain Gym*, teacher's edn, Ventura, CA: Edu-Kinesthetics Inc.

Goswami, U. (2004) 'Neuroscience and Education', *British Journal of Educational Psychology*, 74(1): 1–14.

Jensen, E. (2000) *Brain-Based Learning*, San Diego, CA: Brain Store Inc.

Nummela-Caine, R. and Caine, G. (1994) *Making Connections: Teaching and the Human Brain*, New York: Addison-Wesley.

Organization for Economic Cooperation and Development (2002) *Understanding the Brain: Towards a New Learning Science*, Paris: OECD.

Prashnig, B. (1998) *The Power of Diversity: New Ways of Learning and Teaching*, Stafford: Network Educational Press.

Ravitch, D. (2000) 'Hard Lessons: An Interview', *Atlantic [Monthly] Online*.

Useful websites

Some of the less commercial websites that I have seen (from a range of over three million):

http://eduscapes.com/tap/topic70.htm
http://www.brainconnection.com/topics/?main = fa/brain-based
http://www.fcae.nova.edu/~turgeonm/bbl.html
http://www.funderstanding.com/brain_based_learning.cfm

An extremely comprehensive article entitled 'The implications of recent developments in neuroscience for research on teaching and learning', by Sarah-Jayne Blakemore and Uta Frith, can be found at:
http://www.tlrp.org/pub/acadpub/Blakemore2000.pdf

An interesting, critical article by John Bruer:
http://www.pdkintl.org/kappan/kbru9905.htm

One interesting article on ways of improving learning as a result of brain research:
http://www.league.org/publication/abstracts/learning/lelabs200501.html

CASE STUDY

One important approach used in education and educational research is the case study. A case study is a detailed examination of one person or one setting or one single set of documents or one particular event. Case study focuses on one 'unit'. The unit may be a school (or even a classroom within it); it could even be one student in a school or college; it could be one course; in a study of employers' needs, each 'employing organisation' could make up a single case. This is at once the strength, and, as some may argue, the weakness of case study, i.e. the importance of the context of the unit, and the consequent problem of generalisation.

Bogdan and Biklen (1982) provide useful classifications of case study. They distinguish three major categories: (1) historical-organisational case studies; (2) observational case studies; and (3) the life history form of case study. The first involves studies of a unit, e.g. an organisation, over time, thereby tracing its development. This may involve interviews with people who have been involved with the organisation over a sizeable period of time and also a study of written records.

The second category involves largely participant observation of an organisation. Observational case studies will often include a historical aspect but the main concern is the contemporary scene. Finally, a life history form of case study will involve extensive interviews with one person for the purpose of collecting a first-person narrative.

Stake (1995) made a useful distinction between three types of case study:

1   *the intrinsic case study*: undertaken in order to gain a better understanding of this particular case: not because the case is unique or typical but because it is of interest in itself;

2   *the instrumental case study*: used to provide insight into a particular issue or to clarify a hypothesis. The actual case is secondary – its aim is to develop our understanding and knowledge of something else;

3   *the collective case study*: the study of a number of different cases. The cases may have similar or dissimilar characteristics but they are chosen in order that theories can be generated about a larger collection of cases. In this way, they employ a very different mode of thinking from the single case study.

A case study may well involve a wide range of methods or 'tools':

1   *Observation*:
    (a) *participant observation*: the researcher is more than a passive observer and participates in the events being studied;
    (b) *systematic observation*: use of a standardised observation instrument;
    (c) *simple observation*: passive unobtrusive observation (e.g. of facial expression; language use; behaviour).

2   *Interview*:
    (a) *structured interview*: using a set of pre-determined questions in a set order;
    (b) *focused/semi-structured interview*: using an interview schedule specifying key areas but in no fixed order;
    (c) *open-ended interview*: no pre-specified schedule or order of questions; little direction from interviewer.

3   *Use of documents and records*: includes a wide range of written or recorded materials, e.g. minutes of meetings, pupil records, diaries, school brochures, reports.

4   *A wide range of other techniques*, including: questionnaires; standardised tests (e.g. of intelligence, personality or attainment); scales (e.g. of attitude); repertory grids; life histories; role play, simulation and gaming.

A vast amount of material is likely to be built up in making a case study. Although only a part of it is likely to be presented in a final report, thesis or any publication, it does provide the framework and evidence base for that publication.

Case study research has a large number of attractions and advantages, in addition to the fact that it can be enjoyable to do. Case studies can be illuminating and insightful; if well written, they can be attention-holding and exude a strong sense of reality; they are often accessible and engaging for readers. Case studies derived from research can be of great value in teaching and learning; and case studies can lead *into* subsequent quantitative research by pointing to issues which can or should be investigated over a wider range.

On the other hand, the main problem faced by case study is the problem of 'generalisability'. How far can lessons be learnt and generalisations made from studying just one case or one unit?

Wolcott (1995, p. 17) is perhaps the most 'bullish' in responding to this: 'What can we learn from studying only one of anything?' The answer: 'All we can.' He later elaborates on this by arguing that 'each case study is unique, but not so unique that we cannot learn from it and apply its lessons more generally' (ibid., p. 175).

A similar point was made over 50 years ago by Kluckhohn and Murray (1948, p. 35) in, despite the gendered language, a memorable quote: 'Every man is in certain respects, like all men, like some men, like no other man.' We could add to this: in some ways all schools are the same, in other respects they are all different; similarly for colleges, universities and employers.

Despite the inherent difficulties in case study research (which are also problems for other forms of research), the study of cases is surely a valuable tool, provided its inherent dangers are acknowledged. Perhaps the most important criterion should be that people can learn important lessons from case studies – and *relate to them*. This could be called the criterion of 'relatability' – a far more appropriate notion than generalisability or validity.

References and further reading

Bogdan, R. and Biklen, S. (1982) *Qualitative Research for Education*, Boston: Allyn and Bacon.

Kluckhohn, C. and Murray, H. (eds) (1948) *Personality in Nature, Society and Culture*, New York: Alfred A. Knopf.

Stake, R. (1995) *The Art of Case Research*, Thousand Oaks, CA: Sage.

Wellington, J. (2000) *Educational Research: Contemporary Issues and Practical Approaches*, London: Continuum.

Wolcott, H. (1995) *The Art of Fieldwork*, London: Sage.

Yin, R. (1994) *Case Study Research: Design and Methods*, 2nd edn, Beverly Hills, CA: Sage.

Useful website

http://www.nova.edu/ssss/QR/QR3-2/tellis1.html

CITIZENSHIP

The notion of 'education for citizenship' is a relatively new one in England and Wales though its origins can be traced back to a combination of politicians and educationalists, as far back perhaps as the time of the Ancient Greek city-states. The notion is more widespread than those of us in the UK might imagine, largely because it has different names in different countries. In Singapore, for example, it is referred to as 'national education' or civic and moral education, with similar aims to the citizenship movement.

It has a longer history in the USA than in Britain, going back to the days of the progressive educator John Dewey (1859–1952) and earlier. In the UK, it appeared in the mid-twentieth century and later in UK schools under the label of 'Civics' in some schools. The notion of citizenship has had its critics, not least in being accused of brainwashing or indoctrinating students, imbuing them with an exaggerated patriotism and acting as an agent of capitalism. Attempts to make it part of the National Curriculum (NC) in England and Wales experienced a bumpy beginning. In the early days of the NC it was made one of the five 'cross-curricular themes', in 1989. But it was non-statutory, non-assessed and largely ignored by secondary school teachers who experienced increasing pressure to 'deliver' the statutory subject pillars of the NC – these alone were the only real currency.

Interest in citizenship education was revived after the 1997 election, which saw a huge victory for Tony Blair and 'New Labour'. An Advisory Group, chaired by a former Professor of Politics at Sheffield University, Bernard Crick, was set up. The resulting Crick Report in 1998 identified three key dimensions to Citizenship: (1) participation in democracy; (2) the rights and responsibilities of citizens; and (3) the value of community activity (see their reflection in the three strands below). Similarly, the Crick Report has been described as including three 'heads on one body': social and moral responsibility, community involvement and political literacy. As a result of the political will at that time, citizenship education in England and Wales became statutory, *not optional*, at secondary level in September 2002, occupying 5 per cent of curriculum time. Teachers could no longer ignore it and hope that it would go away (although it remained non-statutory at primary level).

In order to satisfy the demands of the citizenship curriculum (DfEE, 1999), teachers are obliged to ensure that pupils make progress in three areas:

37

1 knowledge and understanding about becoming informed citizens;
2 developing skills of enquiry and communication;
3 developing skills of responsible action and participation.

These are spelt out in detail in the Programmes of Study and can be labelled: knowledge, skills and action (KSA). They can safely be said to be quite demanding – for pupils, teachers and teacher-trainers.

At Key Stages 3 and 4, Citizenship was to be assessed and inspected – and it was not long before Ofsted (the inspection body in England and Wales) had reported and commented on its implementation in secondary schools. Attention by the inspectorate, Ofsted, has ensured that schools have taken it seriously. Yet early reports from inspections showed that the quality of Citizenship teaching 'compared unfavourably' with established subjects and that in 1 school in 4, provision was unsatisfactory (Ofsted, 2005). Some decisions made by senior management in schools were said to be based on 'scepticism'. Schools were not confident about assessing Citizenship and pupils did not 'know what they needed to do to make progress' in half of the schools inspected. One specific problem in these early days of compulsory Citizenship teaching was the problem of drawing a line between 'personal, social and health education' (PSHE) (see **pastoral care and PSHE**) and Citizenship. Ofsted offered a rule of thumb: Citizenship treats as a public dimension what PSHE treats at a personal level. Thus, PSHE is more about personal issues than Citizenship, which is more to do with the context of the person (the community, society and democracy) and action within that context. This may help. Another problem for schools was in identifying and providing good opportunities for pupils to engage in 'responsible action and participation'.

Thus, teachers have been taken to task about Citizenship in their schools, perhaps partly because they have not always taken it to heart. The cynicism shown to civics and citizenship in the past century may still be present in UK schools – especially given the ultimate irony that in a constitution with a monarchy, pupils, on coming of age, will still be 'subjects' rather than citizens.

In some schools in England and Wales, Citizenship has been hijacked by the humanities departments, who claim it as their domain. Subjects such as Science seemed to be ignoring Citizenship in many schools: science teachers may perhaps 'lack confidence' in dealing with controversial issues, while other science teachers feel it as their duty to teach the 'facts' and leave the 'values' to others. My own view is that citizenship is far too important to be left solely to the humanities staff or assigned to PSHE/PSE slots in the timetable. Without a strong contribution from subjects such as Science, the citizenship curriculum is incomplete. One of the main aims of citizenship education in its current form is to produce 'informed and critical citizens' who can 'act responsibly'. Science, and indeed all the subject curriculum areas, each have a unique role to play in meeting these aims.

Views will vary on citizenship, but one thing is certain: the notion of 'citizenship education' and what its aims should be will remain contested and debated. My own view, given the urgent need to protect the planet we live on, is that Citizenship should explicitly adopt a *futures education* perspective. The basic premise of this approach is that 'the school curriculum should encourage pupils to think more critically and creatively about the future' (Hicks, 2001, p. 231). I follow Hicks' view that 'effective citizenship education' should take this stance (ibid., p. 238).

References and further reading

Arthur, J. and Wright, D. (2001) *Teaching Citizenship in the Secondary School*, London: David Fulton.

Davis, I., Gregory, I. and Rile, S. C. (1999) *Good Citizenship and Educational Provision*, London: Taylor & Francis.

DfEE (1999) *Citizenship Order*, London: DfEE.

Garratt, D. and Piper, H. (2003) 'Citizenship and the Monarchy: Examining the Contradictions', *British Journal of Educational Studies*, 51(2): 128–48.

Hicks, D. (2001) 'Re-Examining the Future: The Challenge for Citizenship Education', *Educational Review*, 53(3): 229–40.

Lawson, H. (2001) 'Active Citizenship in Schools and the Community', *The Curriculum Journal*, 12(2): 163–78.

Ofsted (2005) *Citizenship in Secondary Schools: Evidence from Ofsted Inspections (2003–2004)*, London: Ofsted.

Useful websites

http://www.citizenshipfoundation.org.uk/
http://www.citizenship-global.org.uk/
http://www.dfes.gov.uk/citizenship/
http://www.qca.org.uk/7907.html
http://www.teachingcitizenship.org.uk/
    If you want to read more about the history and origins of citizenship, try:
http://cicero.smsu.edu/journal/articles97/massey.html

CLASSROOM ASSISTANTS

Classroom assistants (otherwise known as teaching assistants, 'support staff', 'teaching support' and other names) are adults who work alongside teachers in schools, performing different 'levels' of task. One of the main rationales for the introduction of classroom/teaching assistants into schools was a general belief that teachers could be relieved of some of their non-teaching duties, thus creating more time for teaching.

A recent study in Scotland shed useful light on the value of classroom assistants, how they are perceived and the way they work alongside teachers (Schlapp *et al.*, 2001). The study found that by 2001, most primary schools had been allocated at least one classroom assistant. Successful appointees were usually women aged between 35 and 44 years, who had previously worked in schools as parent helpers, special needs auxiliaries or playground supervisors. Support for teachers and pupils was usually their main role, but many assistants also undertook some whole-school administrative and supervisory duties. Approximately a quarter of all assistants said they would like to undertake teacher training in three to five years' time.

The impact of the classroom assistants was reported on in three areas:

1 *Pupil attainment*: in general, respondents thought that classroom assistants have had an indirect impact on pupils' attainment by allowing teachers to devote more of their own time to teaching. However, since several new initiatives aimed at raising attainment were occurring at the same time, it was not possible to quantify the specific contribution of classroom assistants to this improvement.
2 *The way teachers used their time*: classroom assistants in this study were said to have influenced the way teachers use their time. Most teachers who worked with classroom assistants thought that they now had more time to spend on teaching, planning and managing learning. The biggest practical impact was on the amount of time teachers were able to devote to working with individuals and groups of pupils. Teachers' perceptions also changed: many agreed that they now expected more from their pupils and had more enthusiasm for teaching as a consequence. Teachers also indicated that the presence of classroom assistants allowed them to spend less time preparing resources and doing 'routine' tasks such as registration, handling discipline, and pastoral care.
3 *Classroom interactions and pupils' learning experiences*: the majority of teachers reported that when a classroom assistant was present pupils spent more time on task and experienced more practical

activities and interaction with an adult. Pupils themselves enjoyed working with classroom assistants and appreciated the extra support in the class and elsewhere in school. Pupils were able to distinguish between classroom assistants, whom they saw as 'helpers', and teachers.

Generally, across the UK, the introduction of classroom assistants seems to have had a positive effect in schools. It has affected the way teachers work within the classroom, often allowing them more time to devote to teaching. However, in many schools it is still difficult for staff to make or find sufficient time for teachers and classroom assistants to discuss and plan their work together. This collaboration would certainly be of benefit e.g. in joint lesson planning and preparation; in assessment; in achieving differentiation.

A few other issues have surfaced as classroom assistants have become more prevalent. First, the need for recognised training: many assistants have expressed a wish for better training and qualifications. The amount of training provided for classroom assistants has increased considerably. New National Vocational Qualifications (NVQs) have been made available for teaching assistants. These are work-based, i.e. they are for staff who are already in post and want to prove they are competent in their work or who wish to raise their level of practice to national standards. Candidates are assessed mainly through classroom observation and by examining other things they have done (for example, preparation for lessons). In addition, question and answer sessions and projects/assignments are used to test the candidate's knowledge and understanding of the teaching assistant's role. These NVQs are designed for staff in schools in England, Wales and Northern Ireland (slightly different arrangements apply in Scotland).

Second, the issue of higher-level teaching assistants. In 2004, a programme of 'higher-level teaching assistants' (HLTAs) was launched by the Teacher Training Agency (TTA), said to be introduced in recognition of the contribution that support staff can make to pupil attainment. The government of that time proposed to provide every secondary school with at least one HLTA by 2007–2008. These higher-level assistants would be able to take charge of a class and to cover for an absent teacher (in the USA there are four levels of teaching assistant). There has been some debate between employers of teachers and teacher unions over the role of support staff. Would HLTAs be used to 'take over' some of the traditional roles of the fully qualified teacher? Who will actually be in charge of a class? Will HLTAs really be able to cover for absent teachers? One of the main unions (NAS/UWT) welcomed the employment of additional support staff in schools provided that:

- the role and status of qualified teachers were not diluted or undermined;
- HLTAs worked under the direction and supervision of qualified teachers;
- HLTAs were not interchangeable with qualified teachers;
- regulations and guidance were introduced to define the role of support staff, preventing them from being used as substitutes for qualified teachers, to address current inappropriate use of support staff for whole-class activities and to require that HLTAs meet agreed national standards.

References and further reading

Lee, B. and Mawson, C. (1998) *Survey of Classroom Assistants*, Slough: National Foundation for Educational Research.

Schlapp, U., Wilson, V. and Davidson, J. (2001) *'An Extra Pair of Hands?' Evaluation of the Classroom Assistants Initiative: Interim Report* (Research Report 104), Edinburgh: Scottish Council for Research in Education.

Useful websites

http://www.lg-employers.gov.uk/skills/teaching/
http://www.literacytrust.org.uk/database/teachassist.html#review
http://www.scre.ac.uk/spotlight/spotlight85.html
http://www.specialschool.org/assistant.htm

Excellent advice for teachers on working with classroom assistants can be found at:

http://www.northamptonshire.gov.uk/Learning/Teaching/TeachAsst.htm

COGNITION

This refers to any of the processes that go on in the mind that can lead to the end result of our 'knowing' something. Knowledge may be 'knowledge that' or 'knowledge how', so cognition can include skills and abilities as well as factual knowledge or understanding.

The kind of mental processes that can lead to knowing are numerous, for example, observing, memorising, classifying, pondering, analysing, evaluating, problem solving, imagining, creating, and modelling, and so on.

Cognitive development

Our knowledge and mental skills – our intellectual capacities – develop from birth and this process is often called cognitive development. This process of development is due to a combination of genetics and environment – exactly what the proportions in this combination are and how the two factors interact have long been, still are, and always will be, debated (often called the nature versus nurture debate).

We all differ in the rate of our development, but some psychologists have argued that all humans proceed through certain stages. Jean Piaget, a Swiss psychologist with a background in zoology, suggested four stages of development:

1 sensory motor: the feeling, touching, holding and dropping stage;
2 pre-operational: thinking begins;
3 concrete operational: often ages 7–11;
4 formal operational.

Although Piaget argued that all cognitive development for all children follows this order and no stage can be left out, he did allow that different genetic and environmental factors do affect the speed of development.

Readiness

The idea of being 'ready' to learn something is an important idea in psychology and in everyday life. People often say that they, their children or their pupils will learn something when they are ready to, and when they need to (a need-to-know basis). Piaget stressed the idea of readiness in learning – students of all ages need to be presented with something challenging, just beyond what they know or can do already, but not so complex or difficult that they are overwhelmed and frustrated. This is an important rule of thumb for teachers.

See also: **accelerated learning, Bloom's taxonomy, cognitive acceleration, intelligence, learning theories** and **zone of proximal development**.

Further reading

Some of the classic texts are:

Bruner, J. (1966) *Studies in Cognitive Growth: Collaboration at the Center for Cognitive Studies*, New York: Wiley and Sons.

——(1974) *Toward a Theory of Instruction*, Cambridge, MA: Harvard University Press.

Dewey, J. (1997) *How We Think*, New York: Dover.

Piaget, J. (1972) *The Psychology of the Child*, New York: Basic Books.

——(1990) *The Child's Conception of the World*, New York: Littlefield Adams.

Useful websites

http://chiron.valdosta.edu/whuitt/col/cogsys/piaget.html
http://www.funderstanding.com/piaget.cfm
http://www.learningandteaching.info/learning/piaget.htm
http://www.psy.pdx.edu/PsiCafe/Areas/Developmental/CogDev-Child/

COGNITIVE ACCELERATION

Cognitive acceleration (CA) is based on two premises: (1) that children develop mentally as well as physically as they grow older; (2) that their rate of development with some mental processes, such as cognitive skills, can be accelerated.

CA draws on the theories of learning of both Piaget and Vygotsky. Piaget suggested that there are three main stages of development: from 'pre-operational' to 'concrete operational' to 'formal operational'. Each stage has certain cognitive skills and abilities associated with it. Advocates of CA argue that learners' progression through these stages can be 'accelerated' by certain means. The goal is usually seen as the learner reaching the 'formal operational level' of thinking. At this stage, they can cope with problems involving many variables, as opposed to 'concrete operational' when only a limited number of variables can be dealt with. The underlying drive from CA advocates is that all children should reach their true mental potential – at present, given the existing curriculum and current styles of teaching and learning, many children are not fulfilling the potential that they have for reaching higher levels of development and using 'higher-order **thinking skills**'.

The theory underlying CA is that everyone can develop a general way of thinking that is applicable in many different contexts. This has been called a 'general cognitive processing capacity' (Shayer and Adey, 2002) that is not context-dependent (in contrast, see **situated cognition and situated learning**). This general ability or 'general intellectual function' develops with age and maturity, but it can also be enhanced and accelerated by the right learning/teaching environment and intervention.

Various models of teaching and learning (pedagogy) have been put forward to bring about cognitive acceleration, e.g. observing a peer's successful performance; 'scaffolding' learning; working in the learner's **zone of proximal development** or ZPD. One strategy which uses these and other tactics is the model of pedagogy put forward by the CASE project (Cognitive Acceleration through Science Education), based on five pillars or stages:

- *Concrete preparation*: a task is introduced, the context is set, it is related to previous experiences and the language involved is explained.
- *Cognitive conflict*: new information or a new event is presented that does not fit the learner's existing conception – it poses an element of surprise, a 'mental hurdle'. The learner's existing mental structures (their schemata or the schema in the singular) are challenged. *Equilibrium* is upset – their schemata need to *accommodate* (adapt, adjust) as a result of these new events or observations, in order to *assimilate* or make sense of them (Piaget's terms). This is rather like human vision: our eyes 'accommodate', as the muscles adjust the lens, so that we can see or 'make out' things nearby or at a distance. For cognitive conflict to be valuable, it must be within the ZPD (Vygotsky's term) – this is the region between what a learner can achieve or understand unaided and what they can achieve with help from their peers or the teacher (a mediator).
- *Construction*: pupils develop the ability to make sense of what is going on – this is the difficult step (from conflict to construction). Careful input from the teacher, within the ZPD, is needed in this stage. New concepts and strategies are developed. Small-group discussion can help this process, the 'social construction of meaning', provided that it is guided and supported by the teacher (as a golfer once said, it is no good practising your faults). In short, construction requires both support and scaffolding.
- *Metacognition*: learners think about their own thinking and reflect on the strategies and actions they have used, e.g. how they solved a problem. After doing a task or solving a problem, they should become conscious of their own thought processes – they should make them explicit and bring them out into the open in some way.
- *Bridging*: this is the final pillar. The way of thinking developed in the lesson is linked to other contexts and situations in the curriculum and to real-life contexts. This should enhance **transfer of learning**. The teacher's role is to challenge pupils to suggest links

and to make them clear and explicit. For example, after a lesson involving, say, classification of animals, the same skill could be applied to classifying plants or better still the learner's CD collection, hard disk files, stamp collection or personal documents.

Several large-scale programmes have been active in schools in the past few decades: for example, CASE, CATE and CAME (Cognitive Acceleration in Science/Technology/Mathematics respectively). Programmes for CA in the Arts area have also been developed. Programmes have been applied with a range of ages, at primary and secondary level. Advocates of CA put it forward as a new pedagogic model, i.e. a teaching and learning strategy, with far-reaching positive effects. It requires a shift in teaching and curriculum time away from content and towards general intellectual development. This is sometimes said to be a better preparation for a knowledge, ICT-based society than the traditional curriculum emphasis on content. Another suggestion is that motivation is improved. Evidence has also been collected suggesting that cognitive acceleration of this kind can accelerate pupils' development and even produce better results in national tests and examinations (Adey and Shayer, 1994; Shayer and Adey, 2002).

An idea related to cognitive acceleration is that of Instrumental Enrichment (IE), based on the work of Israeli psychologist Reuven Feuerstein, whose programme of intervention is based on the views that: (1) thinking skills can be taught and learned and that these skills are transferable and usable in all areas of life; and (2) intelligence is modifiable and not fixed. The aims of the IE programmes are to sharpen critical thinking, to develop independent learning, and to help students to 'learn how to learn'.

See also: **alternative frameworks, cognition,** and **learning theories**.

References and further reading

Adey, P. and Shayer, M. (1994) *Really Raising Standards: Cognitive Intervention and Academic Achievement,* London: Routledge.

Shayer, M. and Adey, P. (eds) (2002) *Learning Intelligence: Cognitive Acceleration across the Curriculum from 5 to 15 Years,* Buckingham: Open University Press.

Useful websites

http://www.azteachscience.co.uk/code/development/case/cognitive_acceleration.html

http://www.standards.dfes.gov.uk/beaconschools/kingedwa/1002623643/
A company developed in 1999 to promote cognitive acceleration programmes in schools:
http://www.cogprog.com/
For an introduction to Feuerstein's work, see:
http://www.thinkingskillsuk.org/fiep.htm

COMMUNITIES OF PRACTICE

This term is a new name to refer to a centuries-old phenomenon.
The notion is based on the idea that learning involves participation in
a community; the learner's involvement in that community deepens
as he or she becomes more involved in it. It is a useful idea for
schools, colleges, and indeed all organisations where learning is
important (the term 'learning organisation' became fashionable in the
late twentieth century). It is now being increasingly applied to virtual
or **e-learning**: learners communicating with each other and perhaps
a tutor on-line can develop virtual communities of practice. The
model has also been successfully applied in considering
apprenticeships – the new apprentice starts off as a newcomer and is
gradually initiated into the community, eventually becoming a central
member of the group.

Thus new learners in the community start off, in a sense, on the
edge of the group and are said to be at a stage of 'legitimate peripheral participation' (see Lave and Wenger, 1991). As their involvement
gets deeper, they become more centrally involved and they move
inwards from the periphery; they learn the language and the practices
of the community.

The 'community of practice' idea is based on the views of learning
theorists such as Vygotsky, who argued that social interaction, joint
activity and conversation with others are central to developing
knowledge, skill and understanding. Communication, and the community, are the key. Learning is social.

Lave and Wenger called this model **situated learning**: all learning
is located or situated in a community, a context. The knowledge or
skill (the cognition) developed in that context is '**situated cognition**'. It may well be the case that the cognition is so situated and
context dependent that it does not transfer to other situations. They
argue that learning communities are everywhere: at work, at school,
at home, in the youth centre; they exist on the street perhaps, and
maybe among gangs and tribes. Some groups are formal and tightly

organised – others are more flexible and fluid, without clear rules and regulations. In some communities we are core members, in others we are on the periphery.

Wenger (1999) argued that three key features define a community of practice:

1 *what it is about*: its enterprise and purpose as jointly understood by the members (even if not written down);
2 *how it works*: the rules of engagement, either written or unwritten;
3 *what it has produced*: this might be skills, routines, vocabulary or even artefacts and resources – a 'shared repertoire'.

Over time, relationships develop leading to a sense of joint enterprise and identity, and common practices that bind people together.

The notion of communities of practice is perhaps most important in considering the learning that occurs out-of-school or informally. This can occur in clubs, groups, gangs, networks, and associations or indeed in any setting where people can interact and engage socially – either on-line or face-to-face. In many ways a student's learning in these communities – and the recognition, identity and self-esteem they may accrue from them – will be as important and motivating as learning in a more formal setting such as a school. Teachers cannot ignore these communities of practice.

Communities may also have their sinister side. Some can be highly exclusive, restrictive and gender-biased, such as the community of steel workers or other occupational groups. Other groups may exhibit strange practices such as bullying or the initiation 'rites' of some apprenticeships where mechanics are sent to search for a left-handed screwdriver; whilst new members in organisations such as the police or army may have been bullied and victimised for their accent or ethnicity. Other groups depend on their own social or **cultural capital** for their success in having influence and being exclusive (e.g. 'old boy' networks).

The idea of a community of practice is useful when considering the social and the situated aspects of learning, and in considering some of the weaknesses of formal education, but it should not be over-romanticised.

References and further reading

Lave, J. and Wenger, E. (1991) *Situated Learning: Legitimate Peripheral Participation*, Cambridge: Cambridge University Press.

Wenger, E. (1999) *Communities of Practice: Learning, Meaning and Identity,* Cambridge: Cambridge University Press.

Useful websites

http://www.co-i-l.com/coil/knowledge-garden/cop/index.shtml
http://www.ewenger.com/theory/index.htm
http://www.tcm.com/trdev/cops.htm
http://www.tfriend.com/cop-lit.htm
http://www-users.cs.york.ac.uk/~kimble/teaching/mis/Communities_of_Practice.html

See: Smith, M. K. (2003) 'Communities of Practice', *The Encyclopaedia of Informal Education,* available at:
http://www.infed.org/biblio/communities_of_practice.htm

COMPUTER-ASSISTED LEARNING

Quite simply, computer-assisted learning (CAL) has been used to refer to any aspect of learning that is enhanced or assisted by the use of computers (even when it may be debatable whether or not the computer use has actually assisted worthwhile learning!). The term is less commonly used now than it was in the 1980s and 1990s, usually replaced by the term **ICT** (Information and communication technology) in learning. This term is more all-embracing than CAL because it makes clear that communication technology, e.g. e-mail, the **Internet** and on-line discussion groups, or mobile phones and other mobile devices, may be involved (the former may be called e-learning; the latter is sometimes called m-learning).

Similar terms to CAL, also coined in the 1980s and earlier, are CBL (computer-based learning) and CALL (computer-assisted language learning). Newer initialisms, which reflect aspects of e-learning, are CMC (computer-mediated communication), CSCL (computer-supported co-operative learning) or CSCW (computer-supported co-operative work), ITOL (IT-based open learning) and even JITOL (just-in-time IT-based open learning!).

Some of the thinking in the early days of CAL was valuable for classifying the types of learning that could be assisted by using computers. Some of this thinking is still valuable today in considering where the 'added value' lies in the use of ICT; and also in deciding what counts as **authentic labour** in a learning situation. A useful classification of types of CAL was made in 1977 by Kemmis, Atkin

49

and Wright. This identified four 'paradigms' by which students learn through the use of ICT (a paradigm is defined as a 'pattern, example or model' by the *Oxford English Dictionary*). They are:

1 the instructional paradigm;
2 the revelatory paradigm;
3 the conjectural paradigm;
4 the emancipatory paradigm.

The instructional paradigm

The overall aim in this paradigm is to teach a learner a given piece of subject matter, or to impart a specific skill. It involves breaking a learning task into a series of sub-tasks, each with its own stated pre-requisites and objectives. These separate tasks are then structured and sequenced to form a coherent whole.

Computer-assisted learning of this type is now given names like 'skill and drill', 'drill and practice', 'instructional dialogue', and so on. Perhaps its main problem is that in the early 1980s some teachers and others involved in education saw it as the dominant paradigm in CAL. This probably resulted in their poor perception of educational programs and the belief that microcomputers were a 'passing fad in education' like the programmed learning machines of the 1960s.

The revelatory paradigm

The second type of ICT use involves guiding a student through a process of learning by discovery. The subject matter and its underlying model or theory are gradually 'revealed' to the student as he or she uses the program.

In contrast to the instructional form, where the computer presents the subject matter and controls the student's progress 'through' it, in revelatory CAL 'the computer acts as a mediator between the student and a hidden model' of some situation. This situation may be *real*, e.g. an industrial process, *historical*, e.g. Viking England, *theoretical*, e.g. the particle theory of matter, or even *imaginary*, e.g. a city of the future. The revelatory paradigm is still exemplified in educational programs by numerous simulations of various types.

The conjectural paradigm

This third category involves increasing control by the student over the computer by allowing students to manipulate and test their own ideas and hypotheses, e.g. by modelling. Modelling must be distinguished from simulation. Every simulation involves using a simplified representation, i.e. a model, of some situation, but in a simulation the model is ready-created by the programmer. The user can then alter and experiment with the external conditions and variables affecting the model, but cannot tamper with the model itself, i.e. internal conditions. In modelling, however, the user creates a model of the situation himself and then may go on to test it, for example by seeing how well it represents and predicts reality.

The potential of model building and model testing is still being increasingly explored in ICT use in learning and particularly in science and technology courses. A model can be formed of some physical phenomenon, e.g. the expansion of a liquid, the motion of a projectile. The patterns predicted by the model could then be compared, say, with the results of an experiment. Clearly, this involves far more control by the learner over the computer. A similar modelling exercise could be used in history, e.g. by studying data in a local census, searching for patterns and forming hypotheses. These hypotheses could then be tested by studying further data, and searching for new evidence in their support. Encouraging pupils to create, use and test their own models can have great educational value.

The emancipatory paradigm

The fourth and final paradigm involves using a computer as a labour-saving device, a tool that relieves mental drudgery. As such, it can be used for calculating, for tabulating data, for statistical analysis, or even for drawing graphs. In this type of CAL the learner uses the computer as and when he or she wants to as an unintelligent, tedium-relieving slave in aiding his or her learning task. This paradigm relates to the distinction made in another entry between *authentic* and *inauthentic* labour. The authentic labour is the central, indispensable part of the learning task. The inauthentic labour is not an integral part, nor is it valued for its own sake, but is still necessary, e.g. doing endless calculations, searching through a filing cabinet, sorting information into alphabetical order, making a bibliographic search, etc. The distinction is not always an easy one to make. Doing calculations may be seen as a worthwhile exercise in itself. But where the distinction can be made, the computer *can* be seen as a useful tool, e.g. in handling information in a history lesson. The fourth type of CAL is perhaps unique in two ways: first, it uses the computer purely as a tool for the learner's convenience, to be used when and where it is needed; second, the computer is only partly involved in the learning process, i.e. to take over the 'inauthentic' part of the learning task.

These paradigms have stood the test of time and are still valuable today in evaluating and looking critically at the use of ICT in learning situations.

See also: **e-learning**, **ICT**, and the **Internet.**

References and further reading

Collins, J., Hammond, M. and Wellington, J. (1997) *Teaching and Learning with Multimedia*, London: Routledge.

Cuban, L. (1986) *Teachers and Machines: The Classroom Use of Technology since 1920*, New York: Teachers College Press.

——(2001) *Oversold and Underused: Computers in the Classroom*, Cambridge, MA: Harvard University Press.

Hammond, M. (1994) 'Measuring the Impact of IT on Learning', *Journal of Computer Assisted Learning*, 10: 251–60.

Kemmis, S., Atkin, M. and Wright, S. (1977) *How Do Students Learn?* (Occasional Paper No. 5), Norwich: CARE, University of East Anglia.

Kerawalla, L. and Crook, C. (2002) 'Children's Computer Use at Home and at School: Context and Continuity', *British Educational Research Journal*, 28 (6): 751–71.

McConnell, D. (2000) *Implementing Computer Supported Co-operative Learning*, 2nd edn, London: Kogan Page.

Russell, T. (2001) *Teaching and Using ICT in Secondary Schools*, London: David Fulton.

Selwyn, N. (2000) 'Researching Computers and Education: Glimpses of the Wider Picture', *Computers and Education*, 34: 93–101.

Somekh, B. (2000) 'New Technology and Learning: Policy and Practice in the UK, 1980–2010', *Education and Information Technologies*, 5(1): 19–37.

Wellington, J. J. (1985) *Children, Computers and the Curriculum*, London: Harper and Row.

Useful websites

Information on the *Journal of Computer Assisted Learning* can be found at:

http://home.ubalt.edu/ntsbarsh/opre640c/partX.htm

http://www.blackwellpublishing.com/journal.asp?ref = 0266–4909

This web page has not been updated since 1999 but gives a useful overview of some of the current issues of that time:

http://www.csis.ul.ie/ta-pg/andrewdoherty/

CONSTRUCTIVISM

Constructivism's basic tenet is that people construct or build their own knowledge and meaning as opposed to having it 'given' or 'delivered' to them. Human learning is constructed and learners build new knowledge upon the foundation of previous learning. This view of learning sharply contrasts with one in which learning and teaching involve the transmission of information from one individual to another, a view in which reception, not construction, is central. Two important practical points follow: the first is that learners construct new knowledge and understanding using what they already know. There is no empty vessel into which new knowledge is poured: as a result, students come to learning situations with knowledge constructed from previous experience, and that prior knowledge influences the new knowledge they will construct from any future learning experiences.

To use the vernacular, learners do it for themselves – it is not something that is done to them (note that constructivism is a view of learning rather than a view of teaching, although certain views of what teaching should be are likely to follow from constructivism).

Radical constructivism

In a sense, the notion that we all construct our own knowledge for ourselves could hardly be challenged – how could it be otherwise, if we are talking about 'my knowledge', 'my interpretation' or 'my meaning'? But the idea of constructivism becomes more contentious and radical if it is taken a stage further. If it is argued that all knowledge is 'in the mind' or is constructed by the learner then the debate really begins. Would this rule out the idea of shared knowledge and understanding? What about the notion of a 'body of knowledge' that has been accumulated over a period of time, e.g. 'scientific knowledge'? The philosopher of science, Karl Popper, for example, talked about a kind of 'third world' of accumulated knowledge stored in books, libraries and now the Internet, which has some sort of existence outside the human mind.

Some versions of radical constructivism can certainly be contested, especially if they lead to a kind of 'anything goes' view of knowledge. This is often termed 'epistemic relativism'. Its basic idea is that any way of knowing is as good as any other – no one form of knowing about the world should be 'privileged' above another. Science is no better than astrology. Equally, one person's or one group's knowledge of the world (and their way of knowing and their epistemology) are not superior to that of another person or group. Francis Wheen, who wrote polemically and cynically about 'how mumbo jumbo is taking over', sums up 'epistemic relativism' with the statement: 'The world is just a socially constructed "text" about which you can say just about anything you want, provided you say it murkily enough' (Wheen, 2004).

However, a constructivist approach to learning need not imply a constructivist approach to epistemology (see Solomon, 1994). One of the radical constructivists, Von Glasersfeld (1984), talked in his later writing of constructivism as a theory of *knowing rather than knowledge*. And the opposite position – the so-called 'realist' view – that knowledge is independent of the learner and that knowledge is either true or false depending on whether it corresponds with reality is easily pulled apart. It depends on a naïve view of reality (the idea that something exists 'out there', independently); and a correspondence theory of 'truth', i.e. that knowledge is only true if it 'corresponds with' external reality. This theory of truth begs the question: how can we know if our knowledge corresponds with reality? Thus, a kind of infinite regress is set up.

My own view is that all knowledge must have been constructed by somebody or more realistically by a group of people. Knowledge is not some sort of entity that it is out there, waiting to be collected or discovered (like picking apples). However, this does not imply epistemic relativism, i.e. that all knowledge is of equal worth.

Constructivism in the classroom

One of the key messages for the classroom from constructivist thinking is the (now seemingly obvious) statement that learning requires some *mental* activity on the part of the learner. Physical activity on its own is not sufficient for 'active learning' – the learner must be mentally active too – evidence of the first (behavioural activity) does not always imply the presence of the second. For learning to be *active*, it must lead to re-structuring of the learner's mind (see Piaget on accommodation). This is in contrast to the view of the mind as a *tabula rasa* onto which knowledge is imprinted. Two other points about learning are, in my view, centrally important for the classroom teacher:

1 New learning depends on the existing knowledge of the learner; meaningful learning must start from this. This implies that teachers need to use some strategy to find out where children are, i.e. eliciting prior knowledge.

2   New learning involves learners in constructing meaning. Knowledge is actively constructed by the learner, not passively received from the environment or the teacher.

See also: **alternative frameworks, cognitive acceleration, learning theories** and **zone of proximal development**.

References and further reading

Driver, R. and Easley, J. (1978) 'Pupils and Paradigms: A Review of Literature Related to Concept Development in Adolescent Science Students', *Studies in Science Education*, 5: 61–84.

Solomon, J. (1994) 'The Rise and Fall of Constructivism', *Studies in Science Education*, 23: 1–19.

Von Glasersfeld, E. (1984) 'An Introduction to Radical Constructivism', in Watzlawick, P. (ed.) *The Invented Reality*, London: W. W. Norton & Co.

Wheen, F (2004) *How Mumbo-jumbo conquered the World*, London: Fourth Estate.

Useful websites

http://crossroads.georgetown.edu/vkp/resources/glossary/constructivism.htm

http://www.sedl.org/pubs/sedletter/v09n03/practice.html ('The Practice Implications of Constructivism', *SEDLetter*, IX(3), August 1996, Southwest Educational Development Laboratory website)

http://www.teacherxpress.com/f.php?gid = 01&id = 34 (written by J. L. Bencze, 2004)

CONTINUING PROFESSIONAL DEVELOPMENT

Generally speaking, continuing professional development (CPD) is the means by which members of a profession maintain, improve and broaden their knowledge, skills and develop the personal qualities needed as a professional. In the context of education, CPD can be taken to mean any activity that increases a teacher's skills, knowledge or understanding. CPD may be informal, e.g. an activity that a teacher engages in during his or her own time, such as visiting a museum, reading a book or watching a relevant television programme, or it could be formal, i.e. attending an organised course or event. This may or may not be accredited.

One model of CPD is based on *Kolb's learning cycle* (see **action research**). This is a model of learning which involves a continuous cycle of: concrete experience → observation and analysis → abstract re-conceptualisation → active experimentation.

A CPD course may involve an initial orientation, then the course input, followed by a concrete experience which may involve putting the ideas into practice; this leads to reflection and evaluation (did it work?) followed by re-conceptualisation and re-orientation and so on around the cycle.

In teacher education, the provision of CPD is often based on *Shulman's concepts of PCK and SK*. This notion is based on the view that subject teachers have basically two sets of knowledge: their knowledge of their own subject (SK) accumulated during their own studies and perhaps degree course, e.g. in history, science, mathematics; and their knowledge of how to teach and enable children to learn their subject, i.e. their 'pedagogical content knowledge' (PCK). The art of good teaching involves the latter in all kinds of ways:

- an appreciation of how to order and sequence topics in their subject so that a learner can grasp it, in the right conceptual steps, e.g. which concepts come first?;
- a knowledge of how children learn;
- a knowledge of how to break it down and 'pace it' into manageable 'chunks';
- tricks of the trade: using the right metaphors and analogies to explain difficult ideas in terms of familiar ones, e.g. explaining electricity using the water analogy;
- the skill of switching tactics during a teaching session if the learners appear to be 'glazing over'.

New teachers of a subject often begin their career with a good subject knowledge but a limited repertoire of PCK. The links between the two may be weak, shown by the dotted line in Figure 4(a).

As a teacher's classroom experience grows, PCK should develop with time, especially when teachers are prepared to reflect on their own practice and learn from their classroom experience (see Kolb's cycle of learning). The links between SK and PCK become stronger (see Figure 4(b)). With further experience, the two categories may start to overlap so that some elements of SK and PCK are common. Both SK and PCK may well have grown as a result of teaching experience and continuing development (see Figure 4(c)).

CPD can be used both to update subject knowledge, e.g. contemporary aspects of a teacher's discipline such as history or science; and to develop pedagogical content knowledge. With the reflective teacher, the two should grow in tandem.

Another way of classifying CPD has been in terms of different *types of professional development*:

- *instructional*, e.g. on teaching methods, technology, curriculum;
- *organisational*, e.g. team work, management, decision-making;
- *personal*, e.g. interpersonal skills, career building;
- *informal*, e.g. school culture/ethos, being in a strong, supportive environment versus formal, i.e. courses and activities.

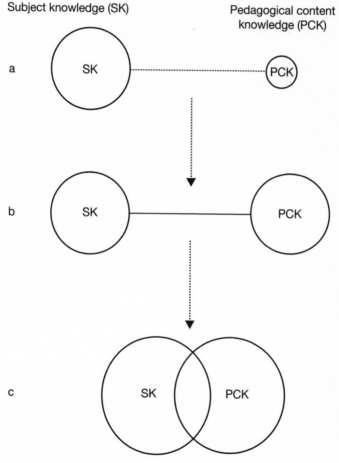

Figure 4 Connection between SK and PCK

There have certainly been tensions in CPD, for example, between individual needs and those of the organisation (the school); and between the drive for accountability and the drive for personal, professional development of a teacher. Equally there have been important trends in CPD since the late twentieth century:

- from externally controlled to school-based or school-focused;
- from 'remedial' to developmental;
- from no strategy to being part of the 'school plan';
- from an individual focus only to group and individual focus;
- involvement of all staff, not just teachers;
- from staff being passive 'recipients' of CPD to staff being actively involved in constructing and shaping it;
- from extrinsic motivation to being involved in CPD to intrinsic;
- from one-off inputs/lectures to various activities including workshops, coaching and quality circles, in a cycle of development.

Research on CPD and its impact has shown that one-off courses (especially away from the school context) have had little impact on actual classroom practice. For example, Joyce and Showers (1988) have shown the vital importance of feedback, coaching and support in developing a teacher's practice. CPD will be of vital importance for both teachers and **classroom assistants** in maintaining the quality, morale and numbers in the teaching profession in the changing times of the twenty-first century.

References and further reading

Harland, J. and Kinder, K. (1997) 'Teachers' Continuing Professional Development: Framing a Model of Outcomes', *British Journal of In-Service Education*, 23(1): 71–84.

Joyce, B. and Showers, B. (1988) *Student Achievement through Staff Development*, White Plains, NY: Longman.

Shulman, L. (1986) 'Those Who Understand: Knowledge Growth in Teaching', *Educational Researcher*, 15(2): 4–14.

——(1987) 'Knowledge and Teaching: Foundations of the New Reform', *Harvard Educational Review*, 57: 1–22.

Useful websites

http://www.msu.edu/~dugganha/PCK.htm
http://wwwpsy.uni-muenster.de/inst3/AEbromme/web/veroef/1995/Bromme2.htm
http://www.teachernet.gov.uk/professionaldevelopment/

CONTROVERSIAL ISSUES

Controversial issues involve topics which are sensitive, publicly debated and on which there is no general consensus of values, attitudes or beliefs. For a controversial issue to be considered important enough to be in the curriculum, my view is that it must:

1 involve value judgements so that it cannot be settled by facts, evidence or experiment alone;
2 be considered to be important by an appreciable number of people and be a key issue for society and the citizens in that society. This would rule out disputes that are purely mathematical or scientific controversies with no impact on society or citizenship; it would also exclude controversies that are simply a matter of taste.

So the decision on what to include as controversial issues is itself controversial but the list of topics is likely to include:

- sex and sexuality: birth control, abortion, homosexuality, and 'permissive' attitudes towards sex;
- energy use and climate change: global warming, transport and energy consumption, international agreements on climate change, energy-greedy countries;
- drugs: drug use and drug abuse;
- nuclear issues: nuclear power, nuclear weapons, nuclear disarmament, peace;
- religion/science conflicts: origins of the universe, creationism and evolution, genetic engineering, the concept of racial superiority, e.g. a 'royal family';
- food and diet: GM foods, vegetarianism, obesity;
- health and medicine: use of mobile phones, smoking and the use of other drugs, euthanasia (freedom of choice).

Why should controversial issues be included in the curriculum at all? Wouldn't life be easier, especially for teachers, if we all steered clear of them? One practical answer is that, even if they are ignored in the formal curriculum, they are certain to surface in a classroom full of adolescent pupils for whom every decision and action is based on a controversial issue: their diet, their sexual behaviour, their mobile phone use, their use of the health service, and so on. More formally, the justification for the inclusion of controversial issues is that any education ignoring them (or trying to) would not be worthy of the name – it would be inadequate. A key aspect of education is to prepare pupils to be citizens in a democracy in which they can play an active part and to make decisions on controversial issues, in their personal and public lives. The process of considering controversial issues should aim to develop the skills of weighing up evidence, searching for information, detecting bias, questioning the validity of sources, in summary, a kind of *healthy scepticism*. This must surely be the central aim of any worthwhile education. Equally, the skills of listening to others, discussion in groups and a considered viewpoint should be encouraged. This is all part of citizenship education, which is now a statutory part of the National Curriculum.

There is widespread controversy on how to deal with controversial issues in schools and over the teacher's role. Two of the key ideas are 'balance' and 'neutrality'. Many writers in the 1970s and 1980s argued that the teacher should act as a 'neutral chair': teachers should not express their own viewpoint or personal beliefs – they should adopt a neutral role, accepting all views and opinions. The teacher might exert his or her authority if it comes to matters of *fact* (when this is clear) – but should not abuse his or her position by pretending to be an authority in matters of *value*, least of all expressing his or her own values and attitudes.

At first, this seems a safe approach to adopt and is certainly less likely to get a teacher into trouble with parents or governors. But what if a pupil (as some do) expresses an objectionable, illegal or downright offensive opinion, e.g. on sex, race or drug use? Does the teacher remain silent and patronise racist, misogynist or illegal viewpoints?

The idea of 'balance' is equally a problem. The law in most countries requires a teacher to give a balanced presentation of opposing viewpoints. But how far can this be taken and how many viewpoints should or could be expressed? One North American school states on its website that: 'In all dealings with controversial issues and materials, the Catholic perspective must be included in the presentation and considerations.' Does this mean that the atheist, Buddhist and Muslim perspectives should also be included to create balance? Should the teacher make a case for smoking, or for taking illegal drugs, in order to balance arguments against? It would clearly be impossible for a teacher to present a balanced presentation of every viewpoint, even if he or she was aware or clued up on them all.

My own view is that the teacher can no longer remain strictly neutral in the classroom – he or she may stop short of expressing his or her own personal views and opinions, e.g. on religion, sexuality, drug use, but the teacher cannot remain silent if insulting, illegal or offensive value judgements are made. To do so would be to take a position of 'moral relativism', i.e. anything goes. This also implies that teachers cannot be required to present a balanced set of viewpoints on every controversial issue – not only is that impossible it is undesirable.

Further reading

There is a wide range of literature on this area, with some of the really valuable discussions first published in the 1980s:

Dearden, R. F. (1981) 'Controversial Issues and the Curriculum', *Journal of Curriculum Studies*, 13(1): 37–44.
The paper by Oulton *et al.* argues that many teachers are under-prepared and feel constrained in their ability to handle controversial issues:
Oulton, C., Day, V., Dillon, J. and Grace, M. (2004) 'Controversial Issues: Teachers' Attitudes and Practices in the Context of Citizenship Education', *Oxford Review of Education*, 30(4): 489–508.
QCA (1998) *Education for Citizenship and the Teaching of Democracy in Schools*, London: QCA.
Stradling, R. (1984) 'Controversial Issues in the Classroom', in Stradling, R., Noctor, M. and Baines, B. (eds) *Teaching Controversial Issues*, London: Edward Arnold.
Wellington, J. J. (ed.) (1986) *Controversial Issues in the Curriculum*, Oxford: Basil Blackwell.

Useful websites

The following website includes the following quote:

> Alberta Education recognizes that education cannot remain neutral on all issues or avoid all topics that are controversial. Alberta Education also recognizes that courses of study and education programs offered in Alberta schools must handle controversial issues in a manner that respects the rights and opinions reflected in different perspectives, but that rejects extreme or unethical positions.

http://www.education.gov.ab.ca/EducationGuide/pol-plan/polregs/171.asp
There is a very useful discussion of classroom issues in:
http://www.vtaide.com/png/ERIC/Controversial-Issues.htm
For a discussion of evolution, see:
http://www.parentcompany.com/csrc/teachevo.htm
For two of the many discussions on the Kansas Board of Education's decision to delete the teaching of evolution from the state's curriculum, see:
http://www.cnn.com/US/9908/12/kansas.evolution.flap/
http://www.valleyskeptic.com/Kansas.htm

CORE SKILLS

See: **key skills**.

CREATIVITY

The notion of 'creativity' has been widely discussed in education for a long time: what is it? Does 'creative' mean the same as **gifted and talented**? Can creativity be nurtured? Should it be nurtured? Can it be assessed and tested? Can it be developed in formal education? Or do the formal education and the curriculum prevent the growth of creativity? Is it actually possible to make people more creative?

The first problem lies in defining creativity. Dictionaries tend to link the adjective creative with words such as original, constructive, productive or imaginative. There are many views about the nature of creativity, going back some considerable time (see Guilford, 1950; Sternberg, 1988; Finke *et al.*, 1992); but there is some agreement that the creative process involves the application of past experiences or ideas in novel ways. Berk brings in the importance in creativity of being 'useful and sensible' by defining it as 'the ability to produce work that is original (that others have not though of before) and that is appropriate (sensible and useful in some way)' (2003, p. 345).

Several educators and populist authors in recent years have argued that we can actually foster creativity and make people more creative, by improving their thinking skills. One well-publicised figure in this area has been Edward de Bono. He talked about lateral thinking – a person who thinks laterally shows signs of creativity. One of his well-known activities was to ask children to design a dog-exercising machine. They came up with all sorts of divergent ideas, including many which involved sticks!

Creative ideas do not always (if ever) appear 'out of the blue'. Often a piece of creative thinking can involve a new synthesis or bringing together of disparate ideas. This is part of high-level thinking (see **Bloom's taxonomy**). Creativity can build upon thinking that has gone on before. Several creative thinkers in science (such as Einstein and Newton) have used the analogy of 'standing on the shoulders of giants' in creating their own theories and ideas. Many of Shakespeare's plays were derived from earlier stories and plots – some even argue that he would be constantly in front of the courts for plagiarism if he were alive today. Creativity is also said to involve hard work as much as flashes of inspiration and imagination. Thomas

Edison spoke about genius being 10 per cent inspiration and 90 per cent perspiration.

One of the classic authors in the 1960s, whose work is still worth reading, was Liam Hudson. He talked about 'divergent' and 'convergent' thinkers. He asked students to come up with as many uses as possible for a brick – the divergent thinkers, in his classification, came up with a far longer, and far more creative, list than the convergent ones. Many other tests have been devised for divergent thinking, defined by Berk (2003, p. 346) as 'the generation of multiple and unusual possibilities when faced with a task or problem'. Naming uses for common objects such as a brick or a newspaper has been widely used. A more visual test involves asking children to draw as many pictures as they can in a large number of blank circles on a page. Responses to these tests are then scored for the number of ideas generated and their originality.

Critics of such tests have said they are poor predictors of creativity in real life and they ignore the importance of personality and environment in fostering creativity. A more complete view of creativity is called the 'investment theory of creativity' (Berk, 2003; Sternberg and Lubart, 1996). This emphasises the broader context of creativity: the person's cognition, personality, motivation and environment. These factors all play a part in fostering creativity. The following personal factors all play a part: their style of thinking (e.g. the ability to see things in new ways); willingness to take risks; courage of their convictions and their perseverance and patience in following an idea through. As for cognition, it may help to be capable of thinking not only divergently, but also convergently – the latter might involve focusing on the most promising idea or solution, or narrowing down options from a range of possibilities. Creative thinkers are also said to be good at using analogies and metaphors. Also, prior knowledge of a field is vital before a person can contribute creatively to it. Some have talked about the '10-year rule': the idea that a person needs to work in an area or field for 10 years before they can move it forward creatively. Last but not least, the environment for creativity is vital – like learning, creativity is 'situated' and context dependent. There is a long-standing acknowledgement that social processes play a major role in the recognition of creativity (Amabile, 1983). Whether it be in the home, school or workplace, the creative thinker needs time to reflect, encouragement and to be surrounded by others to stimulate and support them. This involves creating the right atmosphere or ethos at home, in school or in a company where new ideas are allowed to flourish (rather like the stories of the creative software and computer companies such as Apple). Part of this can be achieved by the right 'management culture' in a school or a company – a culture that does not militate against creativity.

The value of creativity

Whatever our definition of creativity, there can be little doubt of its value to the personal, cultural, and economic well-being of future society: in terms of new ideas, new art, new design, social progress, new scientific thinking and new inventions. Students do not have to come up with a new symphony, the theory of evolution or relativity to be seen as creative. One of the most widely used and creative inventions in the past few centuries has been the paper clip. It is surely one of the duties of schooling and higher education to promote and foster creativity.

References and further reading

Amabile, T. (1983) *The Social Psychology of Creativity*, New York: Springer-Verlag.

Berk, L. (2003) *Child Development*, Boston: Allyn and Bacon.

Finke, R. A., Ward, T. B. and Smith, S. M. (1992) *Creative Cognition*, Cambridge, MA: Bradford/MIT Press.

Guilford, J. P. (1950) 'Creativity', *American Psychologist*, 5: 444–54.

——(1986) *Creative Talents: Their Nature, Uses and Development*, Buffalo, NY: Bearly Ltd.

Marks-Tarlow, T. (1995) *Creativity Inside Out: Learning through Multiple Intelligences*, Reading, MA: Addison-Wesley.

Osborn, A. F. (1953) *Applied Imagination*, rev. edn, New York: Scribners.

Parnes, S. J. (1967) *Creative Behaviour Guidebook*, New York: Scribners.

Sternberg, R. J. (1988) *The Nature of Creativity*, New York: Cambridge University Press.

Sternberg, R. and Lubart, T. (1996) 'Investing in Creativity', *American Psychologist*, 51: 677–88.

Taylor, C. and Williams, F. (1966) *Instructional Media and Creativity*, New York: Wiley.

Van Gundy, A. B. (1987) *Creative Problem Solving*, New York: Quorum.

Useful websites

http://tip.psychology.org/gardner.html
http://www.bellaonline.com/subjects/3301.asp
http://www.ltscotland.org.uk/creativity/

CRITERION-REFERENCED ASSESSMENT

Criterion-referenced assessment (CRA) measures how well a student performs against a set standard, objective or criterion – rather than how they perform when compared with other students. Put simply, it involves criteria rather than norms (such as average, poor, above average). Thus, CRA measures student skill, knowledge and/or understanding in relation to specific goals, standards or performance objectives. In theory, all students could earn the highest grade if they all meet the established performance criteria.

So assessment instruments can be classified into two main groups: *criterion-referenced* and *norm-referenced*. Some of their key features (including those that are debatable) are summarised in Table 1.

In practice, some of the distinctions expressed crudely in the dichotomy above do not always hold water. For example, it is very hard to take the norms out of criteria – especially when the standards,

Table 1 Comparison between norm-referenced and criterion-referenced assessment

Norm-referenced assessment	Criterion-referenced assessment
Shows an individual's relative standing in comparison to a known group, e.g. class, regional cohort, national cohort or the global age group	A test or type of assessment that provides a measure of performance in terms of a clearly defined set of goals, standards or competences
Is all about comparison and discrimination between students Involves ranking	May help to improve co-operation and lessen the effects of competition Should not compare and discriminate
Is not appropriate for diagnostic assessment	It is harder to 'fail' – the aim is success or 'mastery' for all
It is possible to fail	It should be better for giving feedback to students and helping to inform their future teaching and learning needs
It is said to encourage competition	It is often called 'can-do' assessment in that it shows a student's competences and abilities, i.e. what they can do, rather than what they cannot do It is sometimes called *competency-based assessment*

criteria or goals use adjectives or adverbs such as 'adequate', 'well', 'very well', and so on. The next time you see a set of criteria made explicit for a criterion-referenced assessment, look out for the adjectives in the statements. It is hard to write criteria without norms 'creeping in' occasionally.

Second, in practice it is hard to rule out competition and discrimination in any form of assessment – or to remove the fear of failure prior to a CRA or the feeling of failure after it. Thus, the driving test is, by and large, a criterion-referenced assessment but fears and feelings of failure abound. Third, the use of CRA does not prevent comparisons being made. Children could compare each other in a classroom; international comparisons are sometimes made based on what students in different countries can do, e.g. the ability to add or multiply certain numbers or to complete certain set tasks. Finally, critics of CRA argue that it leads to a lowering of standards (see Atherton's (2002) website) – one criticism has been along the lines of: 'if nobody can fail, is the test worth passing?'

The debate will continue – nothing seems to excite educators, parents, employers and politicians quite like assessment.

Further reading

Linn, R. L. and Gronlund, N. E. (2000) *Measurement and Assessment in Teaching*, 8th edn, Upper Saddle River, NJ: Prentice-Hall.

Useful websites

Atherton, J. S. (2002) *Heterodoxy: Against Criterion-referenced Assessment.* available at:
http:// www.doceo.co.uk/heterodoxy/criterion.htm
http://www.edtech.vt.edu/edtech/id/assess/purposes.html
http://www.teach-nology.com/litined/assessment/criterion_referenced/

CRITICAL PEDAGOGY

Critical pedagogy (CP) has its origins in the civil rights, women's and other worldwide movements in the 1960s and the 1970s. This view of teaching and learning is usually attributed to such figures as Paulo Freire, developed while teaching illiterate adults in Brazil; and also the approach of Septima Clark, the teacher who founded the first freedom schools in the South of the USA during the Civil Rights era and trained many other teachers.

Table 2 Comparison between critical pedagogy and traditional pedagogy

Critical pedagogy	*Traditional pedagogy*
Negotiated curriculum	Imposed curriculum
Authentic, real-life contexts for teaching and learning (rejects distinctions between 'high' and 'popular' culture, and values the latter)	Abstract, disconnected contexts used in teaching (values high culture, dismisses popular culture)
Equal roles for pupils and teachers	Unequal power, teacher in authority
Develops empowerment and social justice	Perpetuates 'oppression' (Freire, 1970) and social injustice
Learners reflect on their own lives and experiences	Students' own lives not considered
Promotes change and action for change	Maintains the status quo
Interdisciplinary knowledge and skill	Discipline-bound and divided knowledge

The idea involves taking a critical look at knowledge, authority and power in teaching, learning and the curriculum. Its main concern is with power and 'empowerment' in the context of teaching and learning (pedagogy). The common theme is the shift in power from the teacher (as an authority on knowledge and the curriculum) to the teacher and students together, as equals. This can be reflected in equal power in decision-making over what is learned, how, in what order and how it is to be assessed. Another aim of critical pedagogy is to provide individuals with the tools to improve themselves and to strengthen democracy, to create a more egalitarian and just society, and thereby bring about social change.

There is a vast literature and a huge number of websites on critical pedagogy (544,000 hits on Google when I searched in 2005). In Table 2, I have tried to give a crude summary of the main differences between CP and what might be termed 'traditional pedagogy' and traditional views of the curriculum.

Another of the key figures in the history of CP sums it up as follows:

[Critical] pedagogy ... signals how questions of audience, voice, power, and evaluation actively work to construct particular relations between teachers and students, institutions and society, and classrooms and communities ... Pedagogy in the critical sense illuminates the relationship among knowledge, authority, and power.

(Giroux, 1994, p. 30)

The notion of critical pedagogy has a long history and an interesting future. It has been said that many aspects and trends in twenty-first-century education – such as student-centred education, new forms of assessment, the negotiated curriculum and differentiation – have their origins in the critical pedagogy movement.

One thing that can be said about pedagogy (teaching and learning) in general is that it is *context-related*. The pedagogy in schools at any time depends on the social context of that period, the political agenda both nationally and globally, the current psychological and educational thinking and the policies of that era – as well as the technology of the time. Thus, pedagogy in Victorian times, with its different social, political, technological and political context is vastly different from the teaching and learning seen now in the classrooms of the twenty-first century.

References and further reading

Paulo Freire wrote a wide range of books on teaching. Although his most popular and influential book is arguably *Pedagogy of the Oppressed* (1972), he wrote for over three decades. In *Pedagogy of Hope* (1994), Freire revisited *Pedagogy of the Oppressed*, and critically examined its main arguments. When he passed away in 1997, he was writing a book on ecopedagogy.

Freire, P. (1972) *Pedagogy of the Oppressed,* London: Sheed and Ward.
——(1994) *Pedagogy of Hope,* New York: Continuum.
Giroux, H. A. (1994) *Disturbing Pleasures: Learning Popular Culture,* New York: Routledge.

Useful websites

http://www.allkidsgrieve.org/Classroom/class4.html
http://carbon.cudenver.edu/~mryder/itc_data/crit_ped.html
http://cleo.murdoch.edu.au/gen/iier/iier2/92p13.htm (Tripp, D., 1992, 'Critical Theory and Educational Research', *Issues in Educational Research,* 2(1): 13–23)
http://www.lib.wmc.edu/pub/jcp/jcp.html (*The Journal of Critical Pedagogy*)
http://mingo.info-science.uiowa.edu/~stevens/critped/page1.htm
http://www.paulofreire.org/ (in Portuguese, with sound)
http://www.21stcenturyschools.com/Critical_Pedagogy.htm

CULTURAL CAPITAL

This is an important idea for secondary education. We usually imagine, or dream of, the possession of capital in the form of money in the bank or under the floorboards, and goods such as the house, the estate in Scotland or the yacht in the Med. But an equally important form of capital in terms of education, status, power and achievement in a capitalist society is 'cultural capital'.

Cultural capital is the capital that people possess by virtue of their status in society, their level of education, their qualifications or credentials, the way they speak, their 'class', their race and ethnicity, where they went to school or university, their connections and networks, their family background. Some argue that it also relates to a person's appearance, speech and accent, attitude and behaviour.

Cultural capital is often transmitted by heredity, though it is not subject to inheritance tax as money and property are. In a sense, it is a well-disguised, hidden inheritance – though it may also be acquired and accumulated. It is sometimes said to reproduce itself, following perhaps the same genetic metaphor.

One of the best theorists on this notion is Pierre Bourdieu, who writes of 'the hereditary transmission of cultural capital' and this 'domestic transmission' as being 'the best hidden and socially most determinant educational investment' (Bourdieu and Passeron, 1977, p. 199). Bourdieu identified three different types of capital: economic, which is basically money or property; social, which is the capital we possess by virtue of our social connections and place in society; and, most importantly for education, cultural capital.

He helpfully distinguished three types or states of cultural capital: (1) the objectified state; (2) the embodied state; and (3) the institutionalised state. The examples below may clarify those ideas:

- *objectified*: material resources such as books, dictionaries, machines (such as computers or other items of ICT) and pictures;
- *embodied*: states of mind, long-lasting dispositions of the mind and body, pronunciation, attitudes and manners, which give the holder bearing and status. Interestingly, dispositions that are given a negative value in formal education – such as dialect, 'street cred', not being a boffin, being 'one of the lads or laddettes' and using in-speech or writing such as texting – may be valued highly in other circles outside formal education (e.g. in street networks or cyber-networks);
- *institutionalised*: this usually refers to credentials and academic qualifications but the following are aspects of cultural capital too:

networks (such as the 'old boy network'), friends (who you know), group memberships (such as the Freemasons), titles, the family name (such as the Churchills), connections, reciprocity or co-operation (string pulling, tit for tat). This form of capital is also 'social capital'; it is determined by, and a determinant of, systems of human social interaction. The larger the network, and the more important or well blessed in terms of cultural capital the members, the more a person can profit from this institutionalised or social capital. According to Bourdieu, the capital is maintained by occasions, such as parties, hunts, rallies or receptions; by practices, such as smart neighbourhoods, select schools and exclusive clubs (golf, tennis); and by practices, such as ceremonies, smart sports (like polo) and games (bridge, perhaps?). These activities serve to maintain and strengthen the networks.

Thus, the first form exists *outside* the individual, the second *inside*, and the third as a result of the *interactions between individuals*.

Of course, cultural capital can be converted into economic capital. This can be by virtue of a person's high-status job, as a result of which they can derive a far greater return from their working time than a person with less status (most obviously in terms of money per hour of labour) but also their spare time may be used more productively and ultimately profitably as a result of social capital.

The value of cultural capital will increase with its scarcity, in the same way as a rare material commodity (such as gold) is valuable because it is rare. Bourdieu talks of the person who can read in 'a world of illiterates'. Similarly, the possession of a university degree is arguably more valuable in a society where graduates are scarce – and the inverse is also true.

Academic or educational success or failure has as much to do with cultural capital as with innate aptitudes and abilities. Achievement depends as much on cultural capital as on education and schooling (what Bourdieu calls 'scholastic investment'). To possess capital is to have power. What appears to be 'equal educational opportunity' may be deceptive. Equally, at the other end, the direct value of educational qualifications is never separable from the holder – a first-class degree from Oxbridge will be worth more in the hands of someone with cultural capital, e.g. through old boy networks, than for a 'high achiever' from the working class.

Thus, the economy of cultural capital is far more subtle than that of money or goods. It is less transparent, well disguised and escapes observation and controls, such as tax. For that reason, social theorists have done a great service to teachers and educators in bringing it to our attention. It is an important concept for education at all levels: some argue that schools reflect more of the social and cultural capital of the middle classes than they do the working class; others, such as Basil Bernstein, have argued that the existence of cultural and social capital makes it almost impossible for schools to compensate for the inequalities that exist in society; and the wide variety of cultural capital in life outside school makes it impossible for students from different social groups to 'compete on a level playing field'.

References and further reading

Bourdieu, P. (1986a) *Distinction*, London: Routledge and Kegan Paul.
——(1986b) 'The Forms of Capital', in Richardson, J. (ed.) *Handbook of Theory and Research for the Sociology of Education*, Westport, CT: Greenwood, pp. 241–58.
Bourdieu, P. and Passeron, J. (1977) *Reproduction in Education, Society and Culture*, London: Sage.

Useful websites

http://www.perfectfit.org/CT/apple7.html
http://www.williambowles.info/mimo/refs/tece1ef.htm

CURRICULUM

What is curriculum? Intention and reality

There has been a long debate over the meaning of the word curriculum. Some have defined it to include *all* the processes (formal and informal) by which learners gain knowledge and understanding, develop skills and alter attitudes and values (e.g. Hass, 1987). This is a wide definition as it includes all the learning experiences and events that students encounter and it involves attitudes and values as well as knowledge. A similar definition was given by Doll (1987) but was narrowed down by saying 'under the direction of an institution of learning'. This would rule out informal learning, e.g. on the street or at home, and also unintentional or undirected learning.

The dictionary tends to define 'curriculum' as (roughly speaking) a course, especially a planned, regular course of study taking place at a school, college or university. This would now be recognised as the *formal curriculum*, i.e. the curriculum that becomes institutionalised in the school (via documents and teachers talking to each other), the textbook and the examination syllabus. This notion of a formal curriculum paves the way for thinking about and discussion on the *informal curriculum*– the aspects of a course of study which are not planned and regularised – and the *hidden curriculum* – the tacit or implicit messages and lessons learnt when students follow the formal or informal curriculum. There is some debate on what 'curriculum' includes: is it only *what* is taught (curriculum content) or should it include the teaching and learning process too, i.e. curriculum process or *how* things are taught and learnt (pedagogy)?

Certainly, the way the curriculum is 'delivered' (a word which became increasingly common at the end of the twentieth century) does affect the hidden curriculum. If we define curriculum to include all the experiences of children when they are in school or college, then it contains many informal and hidden elements, e.g. the experience at meal times or break times. It is far more than the intended, prescribed curriculum that tends to be written down in documents. The same blueprint can result in many different practices and realities. There is a distinction between what is planned, prescribed and intended (what is supposed to happen) versus a mixture of the hidden, unplanned and informal, i.e. what actually does happen:

> For example, through the hidden curriculum, students may receive stereotypical messages about minority groups, and male and female roles, due to messages implicit in a teacher's actions, everyday occurrences in the school, or from textbooks.
>
> (McCutcheon, 1997, p. 188)

Who should determine the curriculum?

Curriculum content in schools tends to be socially valued and high-status knowledge – but who decides what valued and high status is? The question: 'What knowledge is of most worth?' has been debated since the time of the Ancient Greeks.

The debate about the content and determination of the school/college curriculum is as old as the history of schooling itself. Opinions are expressed in sources as diverse as the newspapers, books and academic journals. In academic circles the driving force in the UK in the 1960s and the 1970s came from Hirst and Peters with their 'forms of knowledge' thesis, which formed the staple diet for many an education student. They argued that the curriculum should be based on seven categories of knowledge, e.g. moral, historical, mathematical, each of which had its own unique concepts and characteristics. Subsequent curriculum thinkers devoted an enormous amount of time to shooting these bastions of knowledge down in flames but the debate has inevitably moved on to involve parents, politicians, employers and 'captains of industry'.

Political 'interference' in the curriculum became prevalent in the 1980s, often linked with pleas from industry and commerce for the school curriculum to 'supply them with what they really need'. This is seen as the so-called vocationalism of that period which, interestingly, began in the UK with James Callaghan's (then the Labour Prime Minister) famous speech of 1976. The irony is that the 'right-wing' thinkers of the late 1980s and early 1990s then seemed to draw upon a revitalised version of the forms of knowledge thesis in justifying their own view of a National Curriculum.

Several questions about the curriculum are the source of perennial debate:

- How should the curriculum be determined?:
    - on economic grounds, e.g. what is best for the economy;
    - on philosophical grounds, e.g. 'forms' of knowledge;
    - on educational grounds, e.g. what is best for the learner.
- Who should decide what is to be the content of the curriculum?:
    - higher education authorities;
    - politicians;
    - employers;
    - parents;
    - teachers/educationalists;
    - pupils.
- If more than one of these groups should have a say in the curriculum, which should carry the most weight?
- Should the curriculum be decided nationally; or should it be allowed to vary from one region to another to suit, for example, the needs of local employers; the wishes of parents in different areas; different groups or classes of parents; different groups/abilities of pupils?
- Should we have a 'segmented curriculum', varying from one group of pupils to another, or a set curriculum, followed by all? Where would either of these positions leave some of the key concepts in the current curriculum debate such as 'differentiation', access, and 'entitlement'?

Theorists such as Bourdieu (see **cultural capital**) have viewed the curriculum, i.e. formal courses in educational institutions, as a way of perpetuating and reproducing existing divisions and inequalities in society: 'In highly structured societies, the greater the variety of different routes through the system, the greater the likelihood that the education system will reproduce (or intensify) the existing patterns of inequalities' (Bourdon, 1974). This statement may apply in your own teaching context, although some may view it as too pessimistic a view of formal education.

When does a course become a curriculum?

Most people would consider that a course of study must have form, structure and a sequence or clear order for it to be termed a curriculum. It would probably also need a rationale underpinning it and a means of assessing students' progress. It would need to have some sort of harmony and coherence.

The outstanding writer on the curriculum in the twentieth century, Lawrence Stenhouse, famously commented that a curriculum is rather like a recipe in cookery. It can be looked at and criticised, it can be tried and tested. It can be varied according to taste. Unlike a recipe, however, Stenhouse pointed out that a curriculum worthy of the name should have clear principles underlying its content, its pedagogy, its evaluation, its means of differentiation and its sequence.

Following the move towards a national curriculum, a detailed curriculum would now commonly be expected to have clear statements of aims and objectives/anticipated learning outcomes and these would be fully specified. If this occurs nationally and the specification is given for every age group of content and aims, then it would usually be termed a 'national curriculum'. The form of a national curriculum varies from country to country but certainly the above conditions would probably apply to all national curricula. Some national curricula are more specific and prescriptive than others, perhaps in some cases looking almost like a book of instructions for teachers to follow, or a written prescription. It could be argued that, if the national curriculum document includes detailed schemes of work and even lesson plans for its subjects, and ideas on how to teach them, we are moving towards a 'national pedagogy', i.e. teachers are being told how to teach and when to teach it as well as what to teach.

Other kinds of curriculum

There are other kinds of curriculum being debated at present:

1 *The thinking curriculum*: this is a term coined by Lauren Resnick (Resnick and Klopfer, 1989). Unlike traditional curricula that may teach content and process separately, a thinking curriculum integrates process and content to reflect real-world situations: students are taught content through processes encountered in the real world. Some thinking and learning processes are said to apply across all content areas and all areas of life and thus are generic and transferable: for example, decision-making, problem solving, evaluating, and comparing (see **thinking skills**).

2 *The spiral curriculum*: this is a term coined by Jerome Bruner. It refers to a curriculum that revisits the same topics repeatedly, often at different ages, levels or stages of development depending on the interest and background of the learner. Bruner suggested introducing important ideas to pupils at an early age in an intuitive, introductory way. As the learner matures, the curriculum is designed so that the idea can be re-visited and taken further and deeper at each stage of the spiral, to match the student's intellectual development (see **spiral curriculum**).

3 *The objectives model of curriculum*: this was a view of the curriculum, popular in the 1960s and based on behaviourist psychology. It advocated breaking every course or curriculum down into a series of learning objectives, which could be clearly specified and assessed. The notions of learning objectives and learning outcomes are still popular in many quarters today ('objectives', like so many ideas in education, have a habit of recurring) despite attacks on the idea by famous names such as Stenhouse in the 1970s:

I believe there is a tendency, recurrent enough to suggest that it may be endemic in the approach, for academics in education to use the objectives model as a stick with which to beat teachers. 'What are your objectives?' is more often asked in a tone of challenge than one of interested and helpful inquiry. The demand for objectives is a demand for justification rather than a description of ends ... It is not about curriculum design, but rather an expression of irritation in the problems of accountability in education.

(Stenhouse, 1975, p. 77)

The debate on the curriculum is central in education at all levels: what should be learnt and taught? How should this take place? Who should decide on the curriculum? Should some groups have more 'say' than others? The debate is characterised by disagreement, change, political interference and fashion. One thing is certain: the curriculum debate is certain to continue.

References and further reading

Bourdon, R. (1974) *Education, Opportunity and Social Inequality*, New York: Wiley.

Bruner, J. (1966) *Studies in Cognitive Growth: Collaboration at the Center for Cognitive Studies*, New York: Wiley and Sons.

——(1974) *Toward a Theory of Instruction*, Cambridge, MA: Harvard University Press.

Doll, R. (1987) *Curriculum Improvement*, 4th edn, Boston: Allyn and Bacon.

Hass, G. (1987) *Curriculum Planning: A New Approach*, 5th edn, Boston: Allyn and Bacon.

McCutcheon, G. (1997) 'Curriculum and the Work of Teachers', in Flinders, D. J. and Thornton, S. J. (eds) *The Curriculum Studies Reader*, New York: Routledge, pp 188–97.

Resnick, L. B. and Klopfer, L. E. (eds) (1989) *Toward the Thinking Curriculum: Current Cognitive Research*, Alexandria, VA: Association for Supervision and Curriculum Development.

Stenhouse, L. (1975) *An Introduction to Curriculum Research and Development*, London: Heinemann.

Useful website

www.infed.org/biblio/b-curric.htm (Smith, M. K., 1996, 2000, 'Curriculum Theory and Practice', *The Encyclopaedia of Informal Education*)

DIAGNOSTIC ASSESSMENT

See: **assessment**.

DIFFERENTIATION

This is a term that was commonly used, almost a buzzword, in the 1980s. The idea behind it is that all pupils in a class are different; these differences may be:

- *educational differences*: due to their prior learning, experiences, schooling and family background;
- *psychological differences*: **'intelligence'** (however this is defined), motivation, self-esteem, attitude and self-image;

- *learning styles*: allegedly, different learners have different styles of learning which suit them more than others, e.g. 'holist' as opposed to 'serialist';
- physical differences;
- cultural, religious or racial differences: different values, beliefs, moral standpoints, attitudes, educational goals and general aims in life;
- gender differences;
- social and socio-economic differences: social class, richness of experience, attitude to education.

'Differentiation' is the business of devising a curriculum, planning and devising lessons and schemes of work, and adapting the teaching process in order to meet the learning needs of all pupils. The huge challenge for a teacher is how to respond to and take account of these needs and differences in a full and busy classroom. Every pupil is different. How can teachers 'differentiate' their lessons in order to recognise difference and try to provide the best lesson for all pupils? This is an extremely difficult task and although differentiation has been discussed for over twenty years now, there is no easy answer.

One strategy has been to use segregation of different kinds:

1 *By school*: in the past, pupils have been differentiated by sending them to separate schools at, for example, the age of 11. Separation was achieved by examinations such as the '11-plus', designed to segregate the grammar school pupils from the secondary modern and the technical school pupils (the tripartite system, following the 1944 Education Act). This is less common now but the 11-plus is still used in some areas. Of course, we still have a form of segregation: between state schools, private schools and public schools. This form of division depends on many factors including the parents' socio-economic background, class, social networks, attitudes and willingness to pay if they have the means to do so. School pupils are also segregated by religion in many countries, not least the UK which supports educational provision, for example, in Catholic, Muslim and Jewish schools.
2 *By setting*: some have suggested separating pupils within a year group into different 'sets'; these sets would stay together for all subjects, e.g. from the 'top set' down to the 'bottom set'.
3 *By streaming*: this involves dividing pupils into separate classes or 'streams' for different subjects, e.g. mathematics, languages, science. Thus there will be top streams down to bottom streams for these streamed subjects.

4 *By dividing pupils within the same class into groups*: pupils in primary and secondary schools have been divided into groups for certain activities according to their assessed or alleged ability and attainment. Alternative labels have sometimes been used to disguise this, e.g. using names of fruits such as the 'orange group', the 'apples', and so on, as opposed to groups 1, 2, 3, 4, etc. (but it is often said that the pupils take a matter of seconds to work out the hierarchy).

The alternative to setting, streaming and other divisions is to teach in so-called 'mixed-ability' situations. In this case, differentiation can be of two main kinds:

1 *by task or activity*: providing different tasks to meet the individual needs, learning styles and other differences within the group;
2 *by outcome*: by allowing different results and different outcomes from different pupils according to the activity or task they are given. This will also imply different assessment for different pupils.

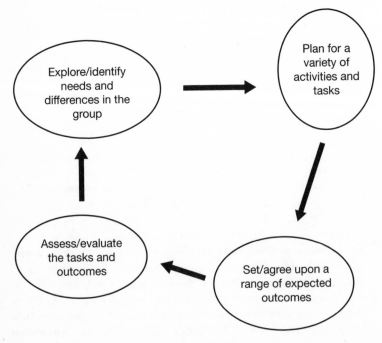

Figure 5 A strategy for differentiation

Again, this is easier said than done. This strategy involves first iden-tifying or diagnosing needs, then planning a variety of tasks to meet those needs, then agreeing on a set of outcomes from those tasks/activities that can be evaluated and assessed (see Figure 5).

To put this into practice requires a huge effort in terms of planning and teaching ability. Planning will require preparation of a wide range of activities and resources; with a very wide range of pupils, the tea-cher may have a classroom assistant and he or she will also need to be involved in planning for differentiation. In teaching itself, differ-entiation requires a wide range of ways of communicating, e.g. speech, writing, images (multi-sensory) in order to cater for all lear-ners and learning styles. Again, help from a classroom assistant will be needed for particular learners with specific needs, e.g. a deaf child. Great care will be needed in pacing a lesson to suit all learners. Finally, for differentiation to occur in assessing the pupils' attain-ments, imagination and innovation are needed in large supply. A truly mixed-ability class, in a school or local authority where inclusion has been taken seriously, may have children ranging from the so-called **gifted and talented** to those with serious disabilities.

The challenge for the reflective teacher, given the movement towards inclusion, is to plan and teach differentiated lessons (by task, activity and outcome) that create interest, enthusiasm, progression and enjoyment rather than resentment, boredom, distraction or obvious streaming within the classroom.

Useful websites

http://www.cast.org/ncac/index.cfm?i = 2876
http://www.dupage.k12.il.us/gifted/differentiation.asp
http://www.shambles.net/pages/staff/Differ/
http://www.teach-nology.com/edleadership/curriculum_development/dif-
  ferentiation/

DISCOVERY LEARNING

The original premise for this notion was the idea or belief that chil-dren could 'discover' knowledge or learn new skills for themselves. The debate on discovery learning is an old one, which has been revitalised with the advent of computer-based learning, **e-learning** and the growing use of **ICT** in learning generally. As I conclude in this entry, it is now widely recognised that 'discovery learning' is most likely to be successful when the intervention and guidance of either peers or a teacher are present.

The first advocate of discovery learning could be said to be Socrates. In *The Meno*, Socrates is reported to have shown how a 'mere slave' could be taught Pythagoras' theorem by careful questioning. This step-by-step questioning leads the slave to the conclusion that the area of any given square can be doubled by constructing a new square on its diagonal. The slave is not told anything but at the end of a series of 'Socratic questioning' is led to 'discover' the rule of Pythagoras (and is probably exhausted into the bargain).

Rousseau's book *Emile* (1762) can be seen as a later example, in which the ideal education for a child is said to be through discovery learning, with the help in Emile's case of an individual tutor. Emile was to learn science by inventing his own apparatus and solving his own practical problems: 'Let him know nothing because you have told him but because he has learnt it for himself.' The child's development was to proceed 'spontaneously', when the child is 'ready for it' (note that this concept of readiness is linked to Piaget's notion of stages of development; see **cognition**).

Many of the US educator John Dewey's progressive ideas are derived from, or can at least be linked to, Rousseau. Dewey advocated learning by experience, a distrust of verbal instruction and an emphasis on the uncertainty and impotence of facts. Doing was seen as essential for knowing, experience was the only source of knowledge.

The advantages of a discovery approach are clear and few would dispute the following: the pupil is active; pupils can decide for themselves the order and pace of learning; learning by discovery allows for individual differences. Pupils are also said to be more motivated, to have improved retention and to have more insight into the process of inquiry itself (Bruner, 1974).

The revival of discovery learning by Bruner and others in the 1960s led to curriculum development schemes such as Nuffield Science, which invited the pupil to become 'a scientist for the day' and used slogans such as 'I hear and I forget ... I do and I understand.'

Many of the tenets of discovery learning were and are most laudable and few would argue with the underlying sentiments. But the discussion did lead to some awkward polarisations, for example, between 'learning by instruction' and 'learning by discovery' – as if the two were somehow mutually exclusive. Thus, learning by instruction was said to be: passive, didactic, teacher-centred, closed-ended and fact-oriented. Learning by discovery was allegedly: active, child-centred, dialectic, open-ended and psychologically based. As with most polarisations, reality is far more complex. The discovery learning movement inevitably invited sceptics and critics. Cynics in the teaching profession mocked the discovery learning approach with comments such as 'Give a child two lenses and 300 years later they discover the telescope.'

More measured critics of discovery learning pointed out several problems. First, not all concepts are learnt by discovery or are derived from experiences – it is often the case that concepts are acquired and then applied to experience rather than derived from it. Concepts help us to make sense of experience (this is a denial of naïve empiricism of the kind advocated by philosophers such as David Hume). Not all knowledge is gained by experience. Later psychologists such as Ausubel argued that some verbal learning could be 'meaningful', provided it relates to what the learner already knows. He used the idea of 'advance organisers' that can be used to structure and organise our experiences but are not extracted from them.

In summary, then, most educators would now accept that there is a place for instruction or at least guidance in learning. Children can discover certain things for themselves but the value of peer group working and careful guidance and support is undeniable. The notion of 'scaffolding', ironically often attributed to Bruner, has also come to the fore. This metaphor is based on the idea that a temporary support structure can be given to learners to bridge the gap between what students can accomplish *independently* and what they can accomplish *with guidance and support* (this gap or zone is often referred to as the **zone of proximal development**; see Vygotsky, 1978).

The importance of interaction between peers, the value of good teaching and the benefit of **communities of practice** for learners are now widely recognised as vital for both traditional and ICT-based learning.

See also: **constructivism**, **ICT** and **meaningful learning**.

References and further reading

Ausubel, D. (1968) *Educational Psychology: A Cognitive View*, New York: Holt, Rinehart and Winston.

Bruner, J. (1966) *Studies in Cognitive Growth: Collaboration at the Center for Cognitive Studies*, New York: John Wiley and Sons, Ltd.

——(1974) *Toward a Theory of Instruction*, Cambridge, MA: Harvard University Press.

Dewey, J. (1997) *How We Think*, New York: Dover.

Piaget, J. (1972) *The Psychology of the Child*, New York: Basic Books.

———(1990) *The Child's Conception of the World*, New York: Littlefield Adams.

Vygotsky, L. S. (1978) *Mind and Society: The Development of Higher Mental Processes*, Cambridge, MA: Harvard University Press.

Useful websites

http://ali.apple.com/ali_sites/ali/exhibits/1000328/Discovery_Learning.html
http://www.csd.uwa.edu.au/altmodes/to_delivery/discovery_learning.html
http://www.cwrl.utexas.edu/~bump/discovery.html
http://scied.gsu.edu/Hassard/mos/2.7.html
  For two good introductions to the work of John Dewey, see:
http://www.iep.utm.edu/d/dewey.htm
http://www.siu.edu/~deweyctr/publications_of_the_dewey_center.htm

DYSLEXIA

This is not an easy term to define. Dyslexia is sometimes called 'word blindness', but this label is too narrow since the word dyslexia is derived from the Greek words *dys* (meaning poor or inadequate) and *lexis* (words or language). It is a specific learning disability that shows itself in various ways through a student's problems in expressive or receptive, oral or written language. So problems may emerge in reading, spelling, writing, speaking, or listening. Every dyslexic is different but the general problem of dyslexics in processing language distinguishes them as a group: the dyslexic has problems in translating language to thought (as in listening or reading) or thought to language (as in writing or speaking).

Dyslexia is not a result of low intelligence. Indeed, it is often noticed in children who have good general ability but who are either failing with academic skills or who have difficulty with spoken or written language, or who are good readers but poor spellers, or who have good literacy skills but below average numeracy, or vice versa. These discrepancies and inconsistent results are the most frequent signs of possible dyslexia in children of primary school age. Teachers often spot a dyslexic child when an unexpected gap appears between the pupil's learning aptitude and their actual achievement in school.

Other important, external signs of dyslexia are that the pupil does the following:

- may hide reading problems;
- may spell poorly and rely on peers or others to correct their spelling;

- avoids writing, may not write as well as would be expected, or may not be able to write;
- relies on memory and, indeed, may have an excellent memory;
- often has good 'people' skills, e.g. may be good at 'reading people' and be very intuitive;
- may well be 'spatially talented'; professions in which dyslexics achieve highly are often said to include engineers, architects, designers, artists and craftspeople, mathematicians, physicists, surgeons and dentists (see website below);
- may have difficulty with planning, organisation and management of time, materials and tasks;
- may have a persistent speech difficulty, or may have had one in the past;
- may have phonological difficulties, finding it hard to distinguish the sounds within words.

Causes of dyslexia?

Different causes have been suggested for dyslexia, mostly relating to alleged differences in the structure and function of the brain. It can occur at any level of intellectual ability and in any socio-economic group (it is estimated that roughly 4 to 5 per cent of the population are dyslexic).

It is worth emphasising that dyslexia can affect people in various ways because the processing problem can be in different functions of the brain. Every pupil with dyslexia is unique, with his or her own strengths and weaknesses.

Media reports

Dyslexia (like **autism**) seems to attract a lot of media interest. It has been reported that many dyslexic learners are creative and have unusual talent in areas such as art, drama, architecture, and graphics, electronics, mechanics, music, or engineering. Dyslexics often show special talent in areas that require visual, spatial, and motor integration.

Helping dyslexics

Individuals with dyslexia learn best when a 'multi-sensory' approach to teaching and learning (pedagogy) is used. This means using as many senses as possible at a time to improve learning: looking (visual), listening (auditory), touching and doing (kinaesthetic-tactile), and saying. In learning the specialist language of a subject, e.g. technology or science, a thorough and deliberate approach needs to be taken, with plenty of opportunities for practice using hands, eyes, ears and speech.

Thus, pedagogy that is multi-sensory is essential for dyslexic pupils in that it employs all styles of learning during a lesson: seeing, hearing, touching, writing, and speaking. Indeed, this is good practice for all pupils. As well as this, teachers need to take account of some of the signs and 'symptoms' listed above, then offer special help and make certain allowances for dyslexic students.

Further reading

Broomfield, H. and Combley, M. (1997) *Overcoming Dyslexia: A Practical Handbook for the Classroom*, London: Whurr.
Keates, A. (2000) *Dyslexia and ICT: A Guide for Teachers and Parents*, London: David Fulton.
Mortimore, T. (2003) *Dyslexia and Learning Style*, London: Whurr.
Snowling, M. and Stackhouse, J. (1996) *Dyslexia, Speech and Language*, London: Whurr.

Useful websites

http://www.bdadyslexia.org.uk
http://www.channel4.com/life/microsites/D/dyslexia/education.html
http://www.dyslexiacentre.co.uk/
An interesting site about famous dyslexics, including Albert Einstein, Winston Churchill, Walt Disney, Cher and Jamie Oliver is:
http://www.dyslexia.f9.co.uk/dyslexia/famous_dyslexics-0.html
http://www.dyslexia-inst.org.uk/faqs.htm
http://www.interdys.org/

EDUCATION FOR SUSTAINABILITY

Education for sustainability (EFS) or education for sustainable development (ESD) are vitally important notions for both formal and informal education. EFS can be related to several aspects of the formal, statutory curriculum: **citizenship**, geography, science, technology, history, economics, and politics (to name a selection); it also relates to informal education and action outside school.

There are several definitions of 'sustainability' and sustainable development. One of the most succinct is: 'improving the quality of life whilst living within the carrying capacity of the ecosystems' (IUCN, UNEP and WWF-UK, 1991, in Huckle and Sterling, 1997). Others describe sustainability in terms of key factors such as efficient use of resources, minimising waste, limiting pollution to levels which natural systems can cope with, giving everyone in the world access to good food, water and shelter, and so on. My own definition of *sustainable activity* is:

> Activity and development that meets the needs of the present without compromising the ability of future generations to meet their own needs. A sustainable society is one that satisfies its own needs without diminishing the prospects of future generations.

Another aspect of sustainability is that it will not succeed unless it takes a global perspective. *Globalisation* has occurred, and will occur increasingly in the future, as a result of the numerous links and interconnections between people, states and societies which make up the world system now – it is the process by which activities, events and decisions in one part of the world have significant consequences for other people, countries and communities in other parts of the planet.

EFS will involve a three-pronged combination of *awareness, critical reflection* and *action*. Students need to be aware that our current way of life is not sustainable – many students (and many adults) do not realise this. They then need to be able to reflect critically on it – what is the problem? Why can't we go on consuming resources and raw materials such as oil at the present rate? What are the alternatives? The third prong is action: what can we do about this, as individuals and in creating different societies, both nationally and globally?

There are two aspects to living sustainably: the first is living with each other, locally, nationally and globally. This involves thinking about and changing our social and political systems. The second is about living with nature, the natural world: this involves thinking about our ecological systems. Both aspects are central to formal and informal education for sustainability and explain why so many school subjects are and should be involved in EFS.

Two versions of sustainability are often talked about: 'weak' and 'strong'. Weak sustainability involves keeping but regulating our existing way of life so that its impact on the environment and other people locally and globally is minimised. This version allows the existing structures to be retained and maintained without radical change; for example, consumerism remains as part of our lives but an attempt is made to achieve 'the greening of consumerism', with a minimum of state regulation and control. For example, private individuals are still allowed to drive large 4x4s, with high fuel consumption and polluting power, into city centres but this is partially discouraged and some tax penalties are introduced. However, free choice and freedom to pollute are permitted; congestion charges in cities are favoured by the government but not imposed, despite strong evidence that car pollution increases illness and death due to breathing-related disease. The strong version of sustainability involves radical changes to our way of life – it offers alternatives to consumerism rather than its 'greening'.

The problem for subject teachers in secondary schools is: what can I do about it, given the constraints of the National Curriculum and the pressures to achieve examination results? There is not an easy answer but many teachers in, say, geography and science are optimistic that they can at least make pupils aware of, and able to reflect critically on, the future and sustainability. There is tremendous scope in informal education for improving awareness, changing attitudes and encouraging action for sustainability.

A related movement is 'futures education', i.e. making a detailed consideration of the future part of formal and informal education. It revolves around the question: 'What is our preferred future?' The basic premise of this approach is that 'the school curriculum should encourage pupils to think more critically and creatively about the future' (Hicks, 2001, p. 231). I follow Hicks' view that 'effective citizenship education' and, EFS in other curriculum areas should take this stance (ibid., p. 238).

References and further reading

DfEE/QCA (1999) *The National Curriculum Handbook for Secondary Teachers*, London: DfEE/QCA.

DfES (2003) *Sustainable Development Action Plan for Education and Skills*, http://www.dfes.gov.uk/aboutus/sd//docs/SDActionPlan.pdf

Furlong, J. (2001) 'Reforming Teacher Education, Re-Forming Teachers: Accountability, Professionalism and Competence', in Phillips, R. and Furlong, J. *Education, Reform and the State: Twenty-Five Years of Politics, Policy and Practice*, London: RoutledgeFalmer.

Hicks, D. (2001) 'Re-Examining the Future: The Challenge for Citizenship Education', *Educational Review,* 53(3): 229–40.

Huckle, J. and Sterling, S. (eds) (1997) *Education for Sustainability*, London: Earthscan.

Lambert, D. (2004) *Education for Sustainable Development: A New Role for Subject Associations?* Sheffield: The Geographical Association.

Meadowcroft, J. (1999) *Planning Sustainability*, London: Routledge.

Ofsted (2003) *Taking the First Step Forward . . . Towards an Education for Sustainable Development: Good Practice in Primary and Secondary Schools* (Her Majesty's Inspectors, HMI), London: Office for Standards in Education.

Panel for Education for Sustainable Development (1998) *Education for Sustainable Development in the School Sector: A Report*, Reading: CEE, DEA, RSPB and WWF-UK.

QCA (2002) *Education for Sustainable Development (ESD)*, London: Qualifications and Curriculum Authority.

UNESCO (1997) *Educating for Sustainable Future: A Transdisciplinary Vision for Concerted Action*, Thessaloniki: UNESCO.

Useful websites

http://www.dfes.gov.uk/aboutus/sd//
http://www.gcrio.org/edu/pcsd/toc.html
http://www.ofsted.gov.uk
The Key Stage 3 DfES national strategy has a range of material on EFS:
http://www.standards.dfes.gov.uk/keystage3/search/?mode = basic_search& pagenumber = 1&d = m-ks3&search_string = education+for+sustainability

E-LEARNING

The term 'e-learning' covers a wide range of applications and processes that involve the use of electronic media (see **ICT**) in education and training. Terms related to it, and sometimes used synonymously, include: web-based learning, on-line learning, virtual learning, computer-based learning, and a host of others, which seem to be coined on a monthly basis. Some argue that e-learning is a sub-set of distance learning, using ideas such as the 'virtual campus' or the virtual school, i.e. students may not physically be attending a school or a university but are effectively studying under its aegis. Contact between student and tutor or student-to-student then takes place via e-mail, the Internet or an Intranet in some way. However, many full-time students (at school and in higher education) use e-learning as part of their course. If students are linked together and work together collaboratively, many now prefer the term 'networked learning' or computer-supported co-operative learning (CSCL) (initialisms such as this seem to be breeding rapidly, for example, CSCGW: computer-supported collaborative group work).

Some forms of e-learning and courses using it are completely 'virtual' and do not involve any face-to-face contact ('f2f', as it is known in the trade). Those employing f2f as well as virtual contact are said to use 'blended learning' (or blended pedagogy if we define 'pedagogy' as teaching *and* learning).

So much for terminology: the technology involved is often known generically as a 'virtual learning environment' or VLE (usually part of a more general 'managed learning environment' or MLE). Typically, a VLE might have three features: a means of 'delivering' (a detestable word, from the Postman Pat school of education) the 'course content'; an administrative area, which might include key dates, a yearly calendar, important deadlines, gentle reminders, and so on; and, third, an area for communication and discussion. The latter should allow both synchronous (i.e. everyone on-line at the same time, like a chat room but possibly using video too) and asynchronous communication (i.e. people on-line at different times, but responding to each other's messages and words of wisdom). A good VLE should allow people to work together and collaborate on activities such as writing assignments, as well as sharing good ideas and useful resources that students have found, for example. Systems such as *Blackboard*, *First Class*, *WEBct* and others seem to be prevalent but are continually being joined by newer technology.

What are the strengths and drawbacks of so-called e-learning? Well, the rhetoric abounds. Advantages are said to include: ease of access, reduced cost, the power to use multimedia in course content, enhanced collaboration and heightened motivation of students (and perhaps staff). The kind of rhetorical words used are '24/7 access' and 'any time, any place, any path, any pace' learning (once nicknamed 'Martini learning' after a famous drinks advertisement). Several of the claims sometimes made by the more zealous advocates of e-learning include:

1 The CURRENCY claim: *All the information will be current and up to date (and trustworthy) because it is on-line.* This is not necessarily true: information from the Internet is only current if it is up-dated regularly (by a human being) or accurate if it is checked, vetted and refereed (by reliable people).

2 The IMMEDIATE AND EASY ACCESS claim: *Learners can access instantaneously all they need at the 'click of a mouse', from the comfort of their armchair.* Again, not always true: the Internet, for example, is rarely immediate, never free and often slow; and for some, e.g. those who live in a large family, access to a phone line and the PC at the same time can sometimes be denied by others in the household.

3　The ANY TIME, ANY PLACE claim: *Similar to claim 2 but with additional hype about '24/7' thrown in.* Learning in any place and at any time is not that easy in 'real life': 24–hour access is anti–social for those who live in families, for example, or for those who have no home computer, e.g. they have to use one at school or college. 'Any place' is fine if you have a portable with a decent battery life and are not sitting next to an inquisitive person on the bus or train who is either a computer fanatic or who pretends never to have seen a laptop before.

4　The IMMEDIATE RESPONSE claim: *On-line learning gives students immediate access to their tutor at all times and questions or queries will receive immediate responses.* Can you imagine this in reality? Tutors might perhaps have other fish to fry; they will usually be tutoring more than one cohort of students; and they also have to sleep, go to the toilet, have holidays or even have social lives. The limiting factor in response times is not the technology but the energy, time and commitment of the course tutor.

5　The HAPPY FAMILY claim: *All the learners in an on-line group form one big, happy family; gender, cultural and other barriers are transcended by the technology. In this happy virtual family all participants have equal worth and all join in; no-one dominates or is rude, scathing, patronising or otherwise abusive to other members, and so on.* Does anyone really believe this? People in on-line groups can get away with murder (virtually, anyway) if you let them. In cyberspace, there is no nodding, head shaking, dirty look, yawning, posture or other body language – how do you know if anyone is actually listening to you? Conversely, how does anyone know if you are listening if you don't 'talk'? And what do you do about 'long monologue man' (perhaps woman) who virtually will never shut up? Or the 'lurker' who never 'says' anything?

6　The MOTIVATION claim: *All students are turned on by e-learning.* There is little evidence for this. Some are motivated by it; some aren't (like any other mode of learning). Arm twisters (sticks) and incentives (carrots) are needed, as with any other course.

7　The AFFORDABILITY claim: *E-learning will be cheaper, more affordable and therefore more accessible.* Again, this has little concrete evidence to support it. In the 'real world', schools and universities have to be financially sound. VLEs cost money to buy, maintain and adequately staff.

8　The OPEN COMMUNITY claim: *E-learning creates an open learning community in which students can engage in dialogues with their tutors or teachers with no boundaries.* This is true if the group have the time, energy or inclination to talk on-line.

9 The SAVING STAFF TIME claim: *E-learning saves the school or university staff a lot of time.* This may be hard to support: e-learning requires just as much tutor input in creating the right learning environment (the VLE), supporting and sustaining it, motivating students and keeping materials up to date as a traditional learning environment.

The reality is that e-learning, like any technology, from the knife to the motor car, can have huge benefits but equally needs to be viewed with a dose of healthy scepticism. For example, 'hidden costs' need to be recognised (phone bills perhaps); access is fine for some but may be difficult for others; the motivation to go on-line may not be universal; course materials in print-on-paper form are sometimes simply transferred to electronic media without the enhancement of moving images, video or audio; and virtual *contact* does not always guarantee *collaboration.*

That having been said, the potential of e-learning in widening participation in learning, in using multimedia to bring dull or difficult subjects to life, and in bringing students who are geographically far apart 'together' is enormous. It is certain to be around for some time, however the technology evolves – but the area continually needs critical and detailed research to assess its advantages and disadvantages and to impartially evaluate the 'student experience'.

What factors make for successful e-learning?

There is growing evidence from research in this field that certain strategies will work and will enhance teaching and learning – just as certain tactics and strategies do work in face-to-face pedagogy (see Lally and Barrett, 1999; Barrett and Lally, 1999). Several factors can be highlighted:

1 *Course design:* it is clearly a big mistake to simply put traditional, paper-based materials 'on-line' and hope that they work in a virtual environment (once christened 'shovelware' because materials are just shovelled into a VLE). Course design for e-learning can and should build 'e-activities' into the curriculum – as an integral part, not as an add-on. These activities, which would encourage active learning, participation and collaboration, will become a feature of the course: an expectation, not an added option. Course

design of this sort would lead to the creation of a community – bringing people together on-line with a purpose.

2 *Starting off*: at the start of any on-line course or module it helps to make clear the structure and timetable for teaching and learning, with a statement of expectations. Students (and tutors) may be anxious to begin with, and this is alleviated if the structure, and what is expected of everyone, are made crystal clear in advance. This structure needs to be available on-line for consultation. It also needs to be reflected in the design of the on-line teaching space, the VLE, being used. For example, a course might start out with an activity in which participants introduce themselves, and say something about their background, or why they want to do the course. The initial aim is to get people talking so that they feel comfortable in the electronic environment, begin to know the other participants and start to feel that the space in which they are working is friendly. Therefore, the learning environment should have an easy-to-find forum, discussion area or space that is dedicated to this activity. It must be secure so that participants can feel that only they will read the postings. The sense of community that is essential in on-line work will then begin to develop. After this introductory phase, as the community becomes established, more demanding academic work can be undertaken.

3 *Providing 'social space'*: it is also important to have a 'social space' in the learning environment, i.e. a place where participants may just drop in and relax with others on the course. Ground rules need to be established for this, depending on the age, culture, ethnicity and general nature of the group involved. Again, this has implications for the design of the environment. The social space might have a friendly, informal name that suits the group, which is not culturally or gender biased.

4 *Tutor presence*: this is another important factor in helping an electronic learning community to become established. Ideally there should be plenty of tutor presence during the early part of a module. During the middle phase the tutor might step back as the group becomes more confident, but still keep an eye on things. Then, as the activity concludes, the tutor's presence will be required again to draw things together. On the one hand, tutor dominance in a group will seriously reduce the participation of the student members; on the other, a lack of tutor presence, especially in the early phase of an activity, may lead to the failure of the learning community to become established.

5 *Different 'tools'*: a range of e-tools can be used to support e-learning. Discussion can be in real time (synchronous, commonly called 'chat') or out of real time (asynchronous, as occurs in e-mail, bulletin boards). Both have their place. Asynchronous discussion can help in developing a set of ideas over the weeks or months of a course. But joint/group decisions are more easily made in real-time chat. These e-tools also provide facilities that are not available in a face-to-face situation. For example, in a real-time chat seminar the tutor can hold conversations with the whole group while simultaneously chatting to individuals in the group, supporting their difficulties and encouraging their participation. This can raise the overall level of participation and the quality of dialogue in the group during a chat session.

Developing these aspects of learning and teaching so that e-learning is a success thus involves a mixture of course design issues and pedagogical issues. The two go together, just as they do in face-to-face teaching. Successful e-learning will involve a combination of group activities, structure, stimuli, cajoling by tutors and peers, and giving people a purpose or a reason to go on-line – this combination of 'arm twisters' and 'carrots' is exactly analogous to the strategies which are needed in more traditional teaching situations.

See also: **computer-assisted learning**, the **Internet** and **ICT**.

References and further reading

A huge range of reading is available in paper form and from the Internet. Starting points on paper are:

Barrett, E. and Lally, V. (1999) 'Gender Differences in an On-line Learning Environment', *Journal of Computer Assisted Learning*, 15: 48–60.

De Cicco, E., Farmer, M. and Hargrave, J. (1998) *Using the Internet in Secondary Schools*, London: Kogan Page.

Garrison, D. and Anderson, T. (2003) *E-Learning in the 21st Century*, London: RoutledgeFalmer.

Lally, V. E. and Barrett, E. (1999) 'Building a Learning Community On-Line: Towards Socio-academic Interaction', *Research Papers in Education*, 14 (2): 147–63.

McConnell, D. (2000) *Implementing Computer Supported Co-operative Learning*, 2nd edn, London: Kogan Page.

Russell, T. (2001) *Teaching and Using ICT in Secondary Schools*, London: David Fulton.

Salmon, G. (2000) *E-Moderating: The Key to Teaching and Learning Online*, London: Kogan Page.

——(2002) *E-tivities: The Key to Active Online Learning*, London: Kogan Page.

Steeples, C. and Jones, C. (2002) *Networked Learning: Perspectives and Issues*, London: Springer.

Useful websites

http://www.e-learningcentre.co.uk/

http://www.e-learningguru.com/

A useful glossary of terms, compiled by Eva Kaplan-Leiserson, can be found at:

http://www.learningcircuits.org/glossary.html

The UK government website on e-learning is at:

http://www.dfes.gov.uk/elearningstrategy/

EMOTIONAL INTELLIGENCE

The concept of emotional intelligence is sometimes given the initials EQ (emotional quotient as opposed to IQ, intelligence quotient) or EI and may also be called 'emotional literacy'. The notion is based on the idea that conventional views of intelligence, concentrating solely on the cognitive, are too narrow. EI or EQ covers two aspects of intelligence: understanding of oneself and understanding of others:

1 awareness and understanding of yourself, your intentions, your feelings, responses to others, your behaviour;
2 awareness and understanding of others and their feelings, intentions and behaviour.

The concept relates to Howard Gardner's conception of multiple intelligences and particularly 'interpersonal' and 'intrapersonal' **intelligence**.

Goleman (1995, 1998) broke the concept down into five domains of EI:

1 Knowing your emotions.
2 Managing your own emotions.
3 Motivating yourself.
4 Recognising and understanding other people's emotions.
5 Managing relationships, including managing the emotions of others.

The National Emotional Literacy interest group (Nelig) has an interesting website (see below). Its aim is to promote and resource emotional literacy, which they define as the ability to recognise, understand, handle and appropriately express emotions.

The concept of EI is said to be based on various theories such as neuro-linguistic programming (NLP). Personally, I remain sceptical about the extent to which the idea is based on empirical research and 'brain science' as it is sometimes called (see also other entries such as **accelerated learning** and **brain-based learning**). Equally, numerous claims have been made for the efficacy of EI in making people more successful and productive in all walks of life (e.g. in management; see websites below), for reducing stress in organisations, decreasing conflict and bullying and enhancing harmony. These may need to be treated with caution, but I think it can be said that the notion has had practical value in considering learning and broadening the concept of secondary education to include more than just the cognitive domain (see **Bloom's taxonomy**). It can be a useful tool for teachers and for learners, e.g. in reflecting on their own behaviour and learning and its value in improving 'parenting skills' has been advocated too (e.g. Gottman, 1997; Coleman, 2000).

According to the OECD (2002), emotional intelligence (EI) is as important, or more so, than so-called cognitive intelligence. This can be justified partly by the view that constructing knowledge is a social process (see **constructivism**) but also by the model of the brain in which the different parts need to work in harmony. For example, the capacity for self-control and co-operation with others become essential for learning.

References and further reading

Coleman, P. (2000) *Smart Talk: The Six Ways We Speak to Our Kids*, Englewood Cliffs, NJ: Prentice-Hall.

Cooper, R. K. and Sawaf, A. (1997) *Executive EQ: Emotional Intelligence in Leadership and Organisations*, New York: Brosset/Putnam.

Dodge, K. A., Pettit, G. S., McClaskey, C. J. and Brown, M. M. (1986) *Social Competence in Children* (Society for Research in Child Development Monograph No. 213), Michigan: SRCD.

Dowling, M. (2000) *Young Children's Social and Emotional Development*, London: Paul Chapman.

Faupel, A., Herrick, E. and Sharp, P. (1998) *Anger Management*, London: David Fulton.

Gardner, H. (1983) *Frames of Mind: The Theory of Multiple Intelligences*, New York: Basic Books.

Gardner, H. and Hatch, T. (1989) 'Multiple Intelligences Go to School', *Educational Researcher*, 18(8): 4–10.

Goleman, D. (1995) *Emotional Intelligence*, London: Bloomsbury.

——(1998) *Working with Emotional Intelligence*, London: Bloomsbury.

Gottman, J. (1997) *The Heart of Parenting: How to Raise the Emotionally Intelligent Child*, London: Bloomsbury.

Higgs, M. and Dulewicz, V. (1999) *Making Sense of Emotional Intelligence*, Maidenhead: NFER–Nelson.

Lawrence, D. (1996) *Enhancing Self Esteem in the Classroom*, London: Sage.

OECD (2002) *Understanding the Brain: Towards a New Learning Science*, Paris: OECD.

Salovey, P. and Mayer, R. (1990) 'Emotional Intelligence', *Imagination, Cognition and Personality*, 9: 185–211.

Salovey, P. and Sluyter, D. J. (eds) (1997) *Emotional Development and Emotional Intelligence*, New York: Basic Books.

Sharp, P. (2001) *Nurturing Emotional Literacy*, Glasgow: Bell and Bain.

Sternberg, R. J. (1988) *The Triarchic Mind: A New Theory of Human Intelligence*, New York: Viking.

Useful websites

National Emotional Literacy Interest Group (Nelig):
http://www.nelig.com

The following website promotes the concept of EQ and espouses its value, sometimes using snappy summaries such as: 'High EQ = low insecurity = more openness':
http://www.businessballs.com/eq.htm

EQUAL OPPORTUNITIES

Every school has an equal opportunities policy. Teachers have a legal and moral responsibility to uphold its principles. The aim of equal opportunities is not equality in the sense of everybody achieving the same, i.e. equal achievement, which could never be realised, but the removal, as far as possible, of barriers or obstacles to educational achievement and success.

In England and Wales, the curriculum guidance issued by the Qualifications and Curriculum Authority (QCA) refers to the importance of securing equal opportunities for pupils. The inspection system, via Ofsted, requires inspectors to take into account the extent to which a school is 'socially inclusive' and ensures equal access and opportunity for all.

The requirements for equal opportunities are underpinned by law. For example, the Human Rights Act, 1998, enshrines the European Convention on Human Rights in UK law. In the UK, further laws forbid discrimination on the grounds of gender, race and disability, such as:

1 The *Sex Discrimination Act (SDA), 1975* (extended and amended 1986), outlaws discrimination on the grounds of gender. Anybody, including children (or those acting on their behalf), may make a complaint under the SDA if they believe they are being discriminated against on the basis of gender. The *Equal Opportunities Commission* (EOC) was created under the terms of the SDA and has three main tasks:
   (a) to work to end gender discrimination;
   (b) to promote equal opportunities for women and men;
   (c) to review and suggest improvements to the 'sex discrimination' legislation.

   (http://www.eoc.org.uk/)

2 The *Race Relations Act (RRA), 1976* forbids discrimination on the grounds of colour, race, nationality or ethnic and national origins. Anybody, including children (or those acting on their behalf), may complain formally under the RRA if they believe they are being discriminated against or receiving 'less favourable treatment' on these grounds. The *Race Relations Amendment Act, 2000*, states clearly the responsibility that all designated 'public authorities', including schools, have:
   (a) to eliminate unlawful racial discrimination;
   (b) to promote equality of opportunity and good relations between persons of different racial groups.

   (http://www.hmso.gov.uk/acts/acts2000/20000034.htm)

3 The *Commission for Racial Equality (CRE)* is the statutory body for securing racial equality. It was set up under the above Act. Its statutory duties are:
   (a) to work towards the elimination of discrimination;
   (b) to promote equality of opportunity, and good relations, between persons of different racial groups;
   (c) to keep the working of the Act under review and to make proposals for amending it.

4 The *Disability Discrimination Act (DDA), 1995* outlaws discrimination in the provision of goods and services against those with disabilities. This Act has some implications for teachers who are, or become, disabled. It has some application to pupils in

schools. Since September 2002 school governing bodies have been under a duty not to treat disabled pupils less favourably, without justification, than their non-disabled peers and to make reasonable adjustments to ensure that disabled pupils are not put at a substantial disadvantage compared to non-disabled pupils. The Act covers admissions, exclusions and education and associated services. Schools are required to plan strategically to increase access to education at school for disabled pupils. This planning duty applies to access to school premises, the curriculum and to written information. See website below.

5   The *Disability Rights Commission (DRC)* was established in 2000. It was established by the *Disability Rights Commission Act, 1999*. The DRC is the statutory body for advising and assisting disabled people in pursuing their rights under the DDA.

Promoting equal opportunity

How can equal opportunities for all be promoted? Will equality of opportunity ever be achieved? Despite the important legislation listed above, which has surely made some impact, it can be argued that complete equality of opportunity will never be possible in a society which is unequal. Different people, families and groups have different access to money and to **cultural capital**. It has been said that schools will never compensate for society. Gender is still an issue in the secondary curriculum, with subjects such as science and mathematics still said to be as 'gendered' as they always have been. Unsuccessful attempts in the 1970s and 1980s to 'attract' more girls into science and technology by making it more 'girl friendly' are looked back on with derision in some quarters. Yet on the other side of the coin, boys' under-achievement at GCSE level has been highly topical for some time now, with girls being much more successful in examinations and coursework at the age of 16.

Hope is often pinned on technology or ICT to help bring about equal opportunities in education. 'Virtual' learning communities are often made up of people from all sorts of backgrounds, or with different disabilities, who might not otherwise meet. ICT may improve opportunity in education because it can remove at least some of the barriers to learning that some groups face, for example, **e-learning** can remove the need to be in a certain location at a specific time. The anonymity of on-line discussions can also encourage those lacking in confidence to participate much more than they would normally do in face-to-face situations. But e-learning requires access to computer technology in the first place and is rarely free of charge, especially in higher education.

The effort to provide equal opportunities for all school students, with its underpinning legislation, looks set to continue well into the twenty-first century but it is still a long way from achieving the 'level playing field' that some had hoped for at the end of the twentieth.

Further reading

Clark, A. and Millard, E. (eds) (1998) *Gender in the Secondary Curriculum*, London: Routledge.

Useful websites

The BECTa site includes the useful summary:

Equal opportunities in education means providing equal access to the learning experience regardless of race, gender, age, sexual orientation, disability, religion, social background, and academic ability, and applies to all groups of communities including ethnic minorities, Travellers, Asylum seekers, Faith communities, young offenders, older people, and those with disabilities or learning difficulties.

http://ferl.becta.org.uk/display.cfm?page = 608
http://www.hmso.gov.uk/acts/acts1995/1995050.htm
http://www.teachernet.gov.uk/teachinginengland/detail.cfm?id = 229

EVIDENCE-BASED PRACTICE

This is a concept which became fashionable in the late 1990s and has remained a buzzword, a mantra even, into the twenty-first century. It is based partly on a medical model of how practice should be (understandably) based on the best available evidence. Thus 'evidence-based medicine' involves the careful use of current medical evidence in making decisions about the treatment of patients. Practitioners use their own personal, clinical experience alongside the best available evidence from systematic, published research. An influential speech by David Hargreaves in 1996 argued that education should follow this medical model and therefore improve the way in which research can make an impact upon teaching practice.

Transferring this model wholesale to education has its problems however. First, teaching is as much a matter of judgement and interpretation as it is of fact (very much as refereeing a sport can be at times). Value judgements are as important in teaching and learning as are evidence and the 'facts'. It is thus a very simplistic model to assume that all we need to do is to collect the 'evidence' (even if that were possible in something as complicated as education) and then deduce the 'practice' from it. There is a gap (as the philosopher David Hume pointed out) between what *is* the case and what *ought* to be done about it – the 'is–ought' distinction as it is often known.

Second, simply presenting a teacher with the evidence and research on an area and then expecting them to change their practice as a result of it is a false expectation. Teachers' classroom practices (whether they are *reflective practitioners* or not – see **reflective practice**) are influenced by a variety of factors – teaching is a complex business. The key factors affecting teaching style and approach on a particular day are numerous and not always based on educational criteria, e.g. safety or classroom behaviour may take priority in some situations. In planning, and at all times during a typical lesson, teachers are constantly involved in decision-making, and often unplanned (reflection-in-action). Some are based on intuition ('sixth sense'), some on tacit knowledge that would be hard to explain let alone put into writing.

Third, equally, teachers' practices are extremely resilient and difficult to shift. Simply giving them research evidence, e.g. on a CPD course, and expecting them to go away and begin to change their teaching practices is naïve. A huge amount of work needs to go into changing and adapting practice – it may require mentoring and coaching for example (see **continuing professional development**). In some cases, change may never occur because a teacher may have good reasons (though not necessarily educational or even rational ones) for not changing their practice.

Finally, the notion also assumes that evidence (or the 'facts') is unproblematic. In reality, research is often disputed – even scientists disagree on many contentious issues such as global warming, the effect of microwaves from mobile phones, GM foods, etc. Medical research, e.g. on the links between the MMR jab and autism, and social science research, are at least as likely to be inconclusive.

Thus, the notion of evidence-based practice is problematic for several reasons – this is not to deny the value of basing practice in teaching and learning (pedagogy) on the best available evidence and research that has been published. Practice can be informed and greatly improved by basing it on research and evidence. But it is important to question the idea that educational practice can be, or ever will be, crudely based on evidence and follow directly on from it. Evidence-*informed* practice is probably a better term.

References and further reading

Davies, P. (1999) 'What Is Evidence-Based Education?', *British Journal of Educational Studies*, 47: 108–21.

Hammersley, M. (1997) 'Educational Research and Teaching: A Response to David Hargreaves' TTA Lecture', *British Educational Research Journal*, 23: 141–61.

Hargreaves, D. (1996) 'Teaching as a Research-Based Profession: Possibilities and Prospects' (Teacher Training Agency Annual Lecture), London: Teacher Training Agency.

Rosen, W. and Donald, A. (1995) 'Evidence-Based Medicine: An Approach to Clinical Problem Solving', *British Medical Journal*, 310(6987): 1122–5.

Simons, H. (2003) 'Evidence-Based Practice: Panacea or Over-Promise?', *Research Papers in Education*, 18(4): 303–11.

Useful websites

http://www.ex.ac.uk/Affiliate/stloyes/cpd/ebp.htm
Details about the 'EPPI'centre (the Evidence for Policy and Practice Information and Co-ordinating Centre) can be found at:
http://eppi.ioe.ac.uk/EPPIWeb/home.aspx
REEL: the Research Evidence in Education Library is the home site of the Centre for Evidence-Informed Policy and Practice in Education, commissioned by the Department for Education and Skills:
http://eppi.ioe.ac.uk/EPPIWeb/home.aspx?page = /reel/intro.htm

EXCLUSION

Pupils can be excluded from school for a range of reasons and these are usually clearly specified in regulations. In the case of the DfES, the categories include: physical assault or verbal abuse towards a fellow pupil or an adult; threatening behaviour; bullying; sexual misconduct; racist abuse; vandalism including arson; theft; or persistent disruptive behaviour.

There are two types of exclusion: *permanent* exclusions and *fixed term* exclusions. Permanent exclusion means that the pupil can no longer attend the school. Fixed term can be for a few days or longer, and the pupil cannot attend school during this time. Parents must be kept fully informed of any exclusions. Once a child has been excluded, the Local Education Authority is obliged to provide alternative education after the 15th day (in England and Wales, at a Pupil Referral Centre).

The number of pupils excluded from school has increased steadily in recent years (said by some sources to be three times the level of a decade ago) and there is growing concern about the number of girls being excluded, though boys are still well in the majority (over 80 per cent). Black pupils are around five times more likely to be excluded than 'white' pupils according to data in 1996. Pupils with statements of special educational need (SEN) were seven times more likely to be excluded (0.98 per cent) than children without statements (0.14 per cent) (Ofsted, 1996).

Contrary to media myth, violence is not a common cause for exclusion (around one in four at most); the major reason tends to be disobedience, not complying with school rules and rudeness or insolence. Another point to note is that schools which are generally good at managing pupils' behaviour are those who make the fewest exclusions.

A broader concept than exclusion from school, but linked to it, is the idea of 'social exclusion': people are excluded from the benefits of society due to their financial status, lack of formal education, social position, health, ethnicity or for many other reasons. They lack social and **cultural capital**. The government has claimed that education is the key to overcoming social exclusion. This claim is supported by many research studies which indicate that learning/education can improve health, community participation, parenting, family life and economic and social life. For many people, the traditional national education and training system has not really met their needs; on-line learning is being evaluated as an approach which may be able to address the needs of certain people or groups who are said to be socially excluded (see website below).

References and further reading

Gordon, D. *et al.* (2000) *Poverty and Social Exclusion in Britain*, York: The Joseph Rowntree Foundation.

Ofsted (1996) *Exclusions from Secondary Schools 1995/6*, London: Ofsted.

Osler, A., Street, C., Lall, M. and Vincent, K. (2002) *Not a Problem? Girls and School Exclusion*, York: National Children's Bureau Enterprises for the Joseph Rowntree Foundation.

Useful websites

http://www.salford.gov.uk/learning/secondary/school-exclusion
http://www.teachernet.gov.uk/wholeschool/behaviour/exclusion/

A study of girls who have been excluded from school:
http://www.jrf.org.uk/knowledge/findings/socialpolicy/112.asp
For a detailed discussion of reasons for exclusion, see:
http://www.npi.org.uk/summ%20exclusion.htm
On the broader concept of social exclusion, see:
http://www.jrf.org.uk/knowledge/findings/socialpolicy/930.asp
http://www.socialexclusion.gov.uk/page.asp?id = 42
http://www.statistics.gov.uk/CCI/nscl.asp?ID = 8247

Can ICT and the Internet help to reduce social exclusion?:
http://www.ru.org/82inayat.html
Overcoming social exclusion through on-line learning:
http://www.niace.org.uk/Research/ICT/overcomingSE.htm
Centre for Analysis of Social Exclusion:
http://sticerd.lse.ac.uk/case/publications/

FORMATIVE ASSESSMENT (OFTEN REFERRED TO AS 'ASSESSMENT FOR LEARNING')

Formative assessment is often referred to as 'assessment for learning'. Summative assessment *of* learning usually takes place at the end of a teaching/learning block. Its aim is to make comparisons between learners and to measure, grade and report upon learning outcomes. Grades may be given based either on: norms (norm referenced assessment) using adjectives such as good, average, excellent; or stated criteria (**criterion-referenced assessment**). In practice, some stated criteria involve normative words such as good or exceptional so the distinction is not always clear.

In contrast, formative assessment *for* learning includes all assessment activities which are intended to shape, guide, modify, adapt, direct and develop future learning. (Assessment for learning can also be used to guide and shape future teaching but assessment done specifically for this purpose is often called **diagnostic assessment**.) The main point is that the focus of assessment is less on measurement and more on learning. It may involve teacher assessment, self-assessment (students assessing their own work) or peer assessment (students assessing each other's work).

The value of formative assessment

Formative assessment is now often termed 'assessment for learning'. One of the key publications which led to the use of this term, and brought about a renewed focus on formative assessment, was Black and Wiliam's (1998) paper *Inside the Black Box*. They undertook an extensive survey of the existing evidence on assessment (over 580 papers or book chapters) and concluded that formative assessment produces significant and often substantial learning gains. In many cases the most marked improvements occurred with the so-called 'low attainers'. Formative assessment, and the use of self-assessment, succeeded in raising the motivation and self-esteem of pupils, especially the lower achievers. In contrast, the practice of giving marks and grades, and of comparing pupils with each other or ranking them, was demotivating. These practices (and summative assessment generally) serve 'managerial functions' at the expense of the 'learning function' of assessment.

Pupils can play a prominent role in formative assessment (Black and Wiliam, 1998; Pryor & Torrance, 1998). Self-assessment involves them in thinking about their own work and their own learning strategies (see **metacognition**). Peer assessment can be valuable because the feedback is likely to be in language that pupils would normally use and the pupil feeding back can also learn from the process. Black and Harrison (2001) present a 'traffic lighting device' that pupils can use in self- or peer assessment. For example, pupils can underline key words in red if they do not know their meaning; in amber, if they are not sure; in green if they are confident they know them. They can then work with a partner to discover the red words' meaning and to check on the amber words. Thus both peer and self-assessment can offer the opportunity for pupil reflection and can encourage autonomy and independence.

Tensions in assessment

The drive for accountability in school education creates a problem. There is often a tension between external, sometimes political and occasionally parental, pressures on schools to implement summative assessment (for example, with the Standard Assessment Tasks (SATs) in the UK) and the desire to improve learning and teaching through formative assessment. An Assessment Reform Group was set up in 1996 to convince policy-makers of the importance of formative assessment (Clarke, 2001). The report by Black and Wiliam mentioned above, *Inside the Black Box*, resulted from this group. Its carefully reached conclusion was that formative assessment and formative questioning produce significant gains in learning and thereby attainment.

Formative questioning

This is a term given to teacher questioning in the classroom that is designed to assess what children know in order to improve learning and teaching. It requires a longer 'wait-time' (Black and Harrison, 2001; Rowe, 1974, who found that the average 'wait-time' was less than one second) than 'traditional' teacher questioning – in order that pupils can think on their own or better still in pairs or small groups about the question. It can be used to gather evidence about (elicit) children's pre-existing ideas on a topic or a concept (diagnostic assessment is a similar term). Some teachers use a 'no-hands up' strategy with formative questioning so that all learners can formulate an answer. A useful practical tool here is the 'show-me board', a small white board that pupils can write on and hold up for the class. Various studies have shown that benefits of formative questioning and longer wait-times include: students thinking rather than jumping in; pupils justifying their answers; whole-class involvement rather than the 'usual suspects' answering all the teacher's questions; and the creation of a supportive environment where answers can be discussed to promote learning and thinking.

Formative marking

Teachers who mark books often see the same comments repeated over and over again in the same pupil's book. Students have clearly taken no note of the comments or used them to improve their learning. This may occur because the first thing they look for is the letter grade (A to E, for example) or the number assigned to it. Formative marking gives feedback to learners which will help them to improve, adapt and modify their own future learning. The term 'feedforward' has been coined to refer to the feedback given to help a student in improving his or her future performance. This is positive feedback, giving guidance on how to progress (and close the 'learning gap' between where they are now and where they are headed; Sadler, 1989). This is best achieved when the comments are not accompanied by a grade or a mark, i.e. comment-only marking.

Of course, feedback of this kind needs to be acted and built upon, otherwise it becomes formative in purpose but not in function (Black and Wiliam, 1998). Effective feedback to pupils must include a recipe for future action (Wiliam, 2003).

To sum up: the debate on assessment, and who or what it is for, is certain to continue. The late 1990s and early twenty-first century saw a renewed interest in assessment for learning, and the resultant drive and activity have already had a marked impact on classroom practice.

References and further reading

Black, P. (1998) *Testing: Friend or Foe? Theory and Practice in Assessment and Testing*, London: Falmer Press.

Black, P. and Harrison, C. (2001) 'Self and Peer Assessment and Taking Responsibility', *School Science Review,* 83(302): 1–7.

Black, P. and Wiliam, D. (1998) *Inside the Black Box: Raising Standards through Classroom Assessment*, London: King's College.

Clarke, S. (2001) *Unlocking Formative Assessment*, London: Hodder and Stoughton.

Lambert, D. and Lines, D. (2000) *Understanding Assessment: Purposes, Perceptions, Practice*, London: RoutledgeFalmer.

Pryor, J. and Torrance, H. (1998) *Investigating Formative Assessment: teaching, learning and assessment in the classroom*, Maidenhead: Open University Press.

Rowe, M. (1974) 'Wait Time and Rewards as Instructional Variable', *Journal of Research in Science Teaching*, 11: 81–94.

Sadler, R. (1989) 'Formative Assessment: Revisiting the Territory', *Assessment in Education*, 5(1): 77–84.

Wiliam, D. (2003) 'National Curriculum Assessment: How to Make It Better', *Research Papers in Education*, 18(2): 129–36.

Useful website

The DfES National Key Stage 3 strategy (the Secondary strategy) places great emphasis on formative assessment/assessment for learning (AFL) and it has probably made AFL more widely known and widely used than has any other publication. Details can be seen at:
http://www.standards.dfes.gov.uk/keystage3/search/?mode = basic_search& pagenumber = 1&d = m-ks3&search_string = assessment+for+learning

GIFTED AND TALENTED

The terms 'gifted and talented' (G and T) are commonly used toge-ther. Most schools have adopted the Excellence in Cities (EiC) sug-gestion that the top 5 to 10 per cent of pupils in any school, regardless of the overall ability profile of pupils, should be identified as gifted and talented, although the Welsh scheme for 'able and talented' children concentrates on the top 20 per cent.

There once was a time when it was felt that gifted and talented pupils would simply progress or 'get on' whatever the educational climate. The view now is that it is important to recognise gifted pupils and to challenge and stimulate them.

The identification of gifted and talented pupils is a contentious issue since there are various definitions of 'gifted and talented'. One widely used definition is taken from the Excellence in Cities initiative and identifies:

- 'gifted' pupils as those who have abilities in one or more subjects in the statutory school curriculum other than art and design, music and PE;
- 'talented' pupils as those who have abilities in art and design, music, PE, or in sports or performing arts such as dance and drama.

The current government's gifted and talented strategy involves two main initiatives:

1 *Excellence in Cities (EiC)*: this provides funding for 1,300 maintained secondary schools and 750 primaries, in 58 local education authorities, most in deprived urban areas, and some of this funding is earmarked for G and T. More widely, the government's plan is for every school and LEA to have a co-ordinator for gifted and talented pupils, even though there is no specific funding for schools outside EiC areas. Many schools now have a policy to support gifted and talented pupils, a G and T co-ordinator, and lists of pupils in each year group who have been identified as gifted or talented or both.

2 *The National Academy for Gifted and Talented Youth (NAGTY)*: this was established in 2002 and is based at Warwick University. Its brief is to offer support to the most able 5 per cent of the school population and their teachers and parents. It is developing its provision, which includes day and weekend courses run at Warwick and longer residential courses held during holidays in a range of subjects, at a number of venues across the country. Both parents and schools have to make a contribution towards the fees for these courses. NAGTY also leads research into gifted and talented education and provides **continuing professional development** (CPD) for teachers.

Have these initiatives made a difference? There has certainly been more money and support for teachers to organise interesting initiatives under the 'G and T' umbrella: for example, theatre visits, Master classes, sports training schemes, musical events, university visits, fieldwork and team building challenges. However, an Ofsted inspection in 2003 reported that:

In schools receiving full inspections, the progress made by gifted and talented pupils is good or better in just over four out of ten schools. Gifted and talented pupils are often not challenged enough by the work they are given. Their particular strengths are poorly identified and they are often given undemanding extension work.

(HMCI *Annual Report*, 2003)

The main challenge for the secondary school subject teacher is to identify the most able pupils in their classes and to use teaching strategies which challenge these pupils. This is part of the general strategy of **differentiation** in the classroom. The terms *extension*, *enrichment* and *acceleration* are valuable in planning for the most able. *Extension* material usually adds depth, *enrichment* adds breadth and *acceleration* adds pace. **Bloom's taxonomy** also helps in thinking about the kinds of questions and the types of tasks that teachers should include in their lesson planning: for example, encouraging the G and T pupils to *apply* their knowledge, to *analyse* findings, to *synthesise* and to *evaluate*.

Certain practical guidelines can be followed by teachers:

1 *Having higher expectations of the most able*: learning objectives for each lesson should take account of pupils' knowledge, understanding and skills and include the higher levels of Bloom's taxonomy. Different or additional, learning objectives should be set for the most able pupils. One way to do this is to use the 'Must/Should/Could' approach in setting aims and objectives for a lesson. Teachers should also be fully aware of the pace of lessons and expect more able pupils to work more quickly than others and to move on to some higher-level work as the lesson progresses.

2 *Asking more demanding questions*: Using questioning effectively is a good way to challenge more able pupils but it is a skill that needs practice. Questions should challenge the more able, for example asking them to clarify their ideas, to improve their explanations, to analyse, to evaluate and to justify. This will involve: planning questions in advance; asking open and probing questions requiring evaluation and analysis, such as 'What do you think about ... ?', 'Why do you think that ... ?', 'How can you justify that ... ?', 'What is your opinion about ... ?' or 'What if?' and sometimes using more advanced vocabulary and more complex language. Once the whole class is engaged in a task, teachers can question selected pupils at an individual level in the same way.

3 *Encouraging and expecting greater independence*: pupils should take increasing responsibility for their own work, gradually make more of their own decisions about their own learning and begin to work more autonomously. Providing an element of choice often spurs pupils on to produce high-quality work and it encourages them to be active learners.

4 *Setting more challenging tasks*: Challenging activities for the most able will include open-ended tasks and questions (at the higher levels of Bloom's taxonomy), which are clearly structured to allow the most able to move ahead independently. One approach to this is to introduce **thinking skills** activities, such as 'mysteries', 'concept mapping' or 'fact or opinion' (also advocated by the DfES through the Key Stage 3 strategy). An essential aspect of using thinking skills is to discuss with the pupils how they approached the task and get them to reflect on the thought processes they went through (see **metacognition**).

In summary, challenging gifted and talented pupils is not just about organising out of school visits, or laying on extra 'Master' classes. It is about planning and differentiating lessons so that classroom activities will challenge the most able. This includes having higher expectations, increasing the pace, asking demanding questions as well as setting tasks which encourage them to extend their thinking and encompass more complex ideas.

Further reading

Eyre, D. (1997) *Able Children in Ordinary Classrooms*, London: David Fulton.
HMCI (2003) The Annual Report of Her Majesty's Chief Inspector of Schools, London: DfES.
Wallace, B. (2000) *Teaching the Very Able Child*, London: David Fulton.

Useful websites

DfES standards sites:
http://www.standards.dfes.gov.uk/giftedandtalented/
http://www.standards.dfes.gov.uk/sie/eic/eicgiftedtalented/
    QCA Guidance on teaching the gifted and talented (in all subject areas):
http://www.nc.uk.net/gt/general/index.htm
    From the DfES National Key Stage 3 strategy:
http://www.standards.dfes.gov.uk/keystage3/search/?mode = basic_search&
    pagenumber = 1&d = m-ks3&search_string = gifted+and+talented
    NAGTY (National Academy for Gifted and Talented Youth):
http://www.warwick.ac.uk/gifted/

Some useful sites from around the UK:
http://www.bgfl.org/services/gifted/default.htm
http://www.devon.gov.uk/dcs/gt/

Acknowledgement

This entry draws upon work by Jane Ferretti, University of Sheffield.

ICT

ICT (information and communication technology) can briefly be defined as the technology used to gather, manipulate or process, store, present, give access to and communicate information. ICT has been used in schools for only 25 years, but many claims have been made about the value of ICT in education: it can motivate and excite learners, increase achievement, allow differentiation and individualisation of learning, increase learner autonomy and independence, provide an enriched, stimulating teaching and learning environment, allow learners to work at their own pace, have a positive impact on standards and attainment, focus student attention, teach important facts and skills, and enhance the learning of difficult, abstract concepts. How justified and justifiable are these claims?

There is considerable anecdotal evidence, not least from practising teachers, to support many of these claims about the benefits of ICT in teaching and learning. ICT has made an impact on schools and school life, with some applications (such as the Interactive White Board) now becoming common in classrooms. But the search for the kind of 'hard evidence' or 'firm data' that politicians yearn for has been rather like the search for the Holy Grail. It has never quite produced the 'proof' and justification that politicians, who have funded the push of ICT into education to the tune of hundreds of millions, have craved (see the DfES 'Impact' studies, in the references). Despite the lack of unequivocal support for these claims, governments throughout the world have forged ahead with the global agenda of pushing ICT into schools.

The introduction of ICT into schools also brought with it many important issues to do with teachers and demands upon them: lack of training, lack of time to learn, lack of access and availability (having ICT when and where they want it); attitude to, or fear of, using new ICT; scepticism about its actual benefits in the classroom; lack of collegial support, e.g. the principal, head of dept.; lack of technical support, e.g. for troubleshooting, setting up; inappropriate software, e.g. with a poor curriculum fit or wrong language level; and danger of unrestricted access to the Internet. Some of these perceived problems have disappeared with time and the increasing presence of ICT throughout society. But some are still real concerns for teachers in schools.

The use of ICT in education has a relatively short history (see **computer-assisted learning**, **Internet** and **e-learning**). ICT has been pushed into schools as a result of three main areas of pressure:

1 *Vocational*: the belief, and sometimes rhetoric, that if students are ICT 'literate' they will be prepared for employment in the twenty-first century.
2 *Pedagogical*: the belief, outlined already, in the ability of ICT to improve teaching and learning (pedagogy).
3 *Societal and political*: dogged determination from politicians to fund ICT in schools, based on an implicit belief in its vocational and pedagogical power; this has often been reinforced by pressure from parents to use 'the latest technology'(at home and school), based on similar beliefs and the knowledge that ICT is ever-present in everyday life and employment.

Of course, these main areas of pressure have raised all sorts of questions about the use of ICT in education, which are certain to recur in the future. These 'recurring debates' and questions mirror the above three areas:

1 *The vocational*: can we ever achieve a match between school ICT and workplace ICT (i.e. industry and employment) in a context of rapid technological change? Can ICT skills be 'transferred' from a school context to the workplace? Should school or college ICT be driven by a vocational imperative, i.e. preparation for employment?
2 *The pedagogical*: what is the added value of technology in learning? What are **authentic labour** and inauthentic labour in the learning situation? How can we measure the impact of ICT on learning and attainment? Can we ever hope to demonstrate a causal relationship between ICT use and enhanced learning and attainment? What effect has ICT had on the role of the teacher and the actual nature of classroom teaching? (See the 'grammar of schooling', Tyack and Cuban, 1995.)
3 *The societal*: how is formal, school use of ICT related to ICT in society? How does home learning with ICT impact on formal

learning, if at all? How have educational policies been influenced by home and society, if at all? Can equality of opportunity with ICT be achieved?

Interestingly, some of the recent ICT debates are mirrored in case studies of technology in teaching in the more distant past (Cuban, 1986, 2001). The past indicates that these debates are certainly unresolved and are likely to recur – whatever the technological, societal or pedagogical context in the future. One thing is certain: technology and its uses in education (and work) will change. But we need to continue asking the same questions. All the recurring debates discussed above can perhaps best be summarised by the continuing, overarching questions: why should ICT be used in education? When should it be used? And conversely, when should it not be used? How can its use be successfully integrated into the curriculum, in its broadest sense? What do teachers and learners actually gain from using ICT?

References and further reading

BECTa (2001) *Information Sheet: National Grid for Learning*, Coventry: British Educational Communications and Technology Agency.

Collins, J., Hammond, M. and Wellington, J. (1997) *Teaching and Learning with Multimedia*, London: Routledge.

Cuban, L. (1986) *Teachers and Machines: The Classroom Use of Technology since 1920*, New York: Teachers College Press.

——(2001) *Oversold and Underused: Computers in the Classroom*, Cambridge, MA: Harvard University Press.

De Cicco, E., Farmer, M. and Hargrave, J. (1998) *Using the Internet in Secondary Schools*, London: Kogan Page.

Dillon, P. (2004) 'Trajectories and Tensions in the Theory of Information and Communication Technology in Education', *British Journal of Educational Studies*, 52(2): 138–50.

Hammond, M. (1994) 'Measuring the Impact of IT on Learning', *Journal of Computer Assisted Learning*, 10: 251–60.

Kerawalla, L. and Crook, C. (2002) 'Children's Computer Use at Home and at School: Context and Continuity', *British Educational Research Journal*, 28 (6): 751–71.

Leask, M. (ed.) (2001) *Issues in Teaching Using ICT*, London: RoutledgeFalmer.

Ofsted (2002) *ICT in Schools: Effect of Government Initiatives, Progress Report, April 2002, HMI 423*, London: Office for Standards in Education.

Russell, T. (2001) *Teaching and Using ICT in Secondary Schools*, London: David Fulton.

Selwyn, N. (2000) 'Researching Computers and Education: Glimpses of the Wider Picture', *Computers and Education*, 34: 93–101.

Somekh, B. (2000) 'New Technology and Learning: Policy and Practice in the UK, 1980–2010', *Education and Information Technologies*, 5(1): 19–37.

Tyack, D. and Cuban, L. (1995) *Tinkering toward Utopia*, Cambridge, MA: Harvard University Press.

Wellington, J. (2001) 'Exploring the Secret Garden: The Growing Importance of ICT in the Home', *British Journal of Educational Technology*, 32(2): 233–44.

——(2005) 'Has ICT Come of Age? Recurring Debates on the Role of ICT in Education, 1982–2004', *Research in Science and Technology Education*, 23(May): 25–39.

A wide range of DfES (formerly DfEE) publications on ICT is available, for example:

DfEE (1997) *Connecting the Learning Society: National Grid for Learning*, London: Department for Education and Employment.

DfES (2002a) *Transforming the Way We Learn: A Vision for the Future of ICT in Schools*, London: Department for Education and Skills.

——(2002b) *Impact2: Emerging Findings from the Evaluation of the Impact of Information and Communications Technologies on Pupil Attainment, Research and Evaluation Series*, London: Department for Education and Skills/British Educational Communications and Technology Agency.

——(2002c) *Impact2: The Impact of Information and Communications Technologies on Pupil Attainment (Strand 1: Attainment) Research and Evaluation Series No. 7*, London: Department for Education and Skills/British Educational Communications and Technology Agency.

——(2002d) *Impact2: The Impact of Information and Communications Technologies on Pupil Attainment (Strand 2: Perceptions) Research and Evaluation Series No. 9*, London: Department for Education and Skills/British Educational Communications and Technology Agency.

——(2002e) *Impact2: Emerging Findings from the Evaluation of the Impact of Information and Communications Technologies on Pupil Attainment (Strand 3: Case Studies) Research and Evaluation Series No. 8*, London: Department for Education and Skills/British Educational Communications and Technology Agency.

——(2003) *Fulfilling the Potential: Transforming Teaching and Learning through ICT in Schools*, London: DfES.

Useful website

The ideal starting point is the BECTa website:
http://www.becta.org.uk/

INCLUSION

The term inclusion is usually taken to mean the full integration of all children within mainstream schools, whatever their needs. However, to the advocates of inclusive education, the term 'inclusion' involves far more than integration.

Special schools began in the UK in the eighteenth century, with the first school for blind children opened in 1791. In 1896 a Royal Commission decreed that education for 'sensory impaired' children should be compulsory and advocated separate provision. The 1944 Education Act defined 11 categories of special education to meet other needs such as physical or 'mental problems' or 'maladjustment'. A major turning point is often said to be the 1978 Warnock Report which recommended that the term 'special educational needs' (SEN) should replace the 11 categories of 'handicap' listed in the 1944 Act (e.g. blind, deaf, delicate, educationally subnormal, maladjusted). The term 'SEN' is still used by many teachers and educators.

Subsequently, however, the Warnock Report, and the 1981 Education Act that followed, were criticised for not going far enough and failing to fully promote the rights of children excluded from mainstream schools. It was felt that segregation and labelling of children would and did continue, leading to continued exclusion and limited expectations and opportunities.

Full inclusion was seen as the next, desired step – a step further than the 'integration' put forward in the Warnock Report. Inclusion can be defined as the full participation of all pupils in the curriculum and the community of mainstream, local education, i.e. the school changes to accommodate the child, rather than vice versa. The local element is often stressed as a contrast to the time when many 'special needs' children were transported to schools well outside their own neighbourhood and locality, reducing their chances of becoming part of the community around the school.

Full inclusion in mainstream schools is now widely recognised as a desirable goal. But in practice it requires energy, commitment and resources to fully attain. Key factors for inclusion to be realised would seem to be:

- the ethos, atmosphere or climate of the school, including its non-teaching staff;
- the attitudes of teachers, non-teachers, parents and pupils – and the local community;
- classroom support for children with special needs from Learning Support Assistants (LSAs) or similar;
- a common curriculum for all, but with appropriate differentiation;
- a collaborative learning and teaching atmosphere, i.e. children working together; teachers, classroom assistants and other professionals such as speech and language therapists and educational psychologists collaborating and co-operating.

In reality, this has proved hard to achieve, not least due to lack of appropriate funding and other, often conflicting demands on teachers and schools, e.g. to raise their ranking in the exam and test results 'league tables'. Ironically, one of the most publicised criticisms of the problems of inclusion in real schools came from Mary Warnock herself in June 2005, see website below.

Further reading

Apple, M. (1982) *Education and Power*, London: Routledge and Kegan Paul.

Barton, L. (1997) 'The Politics of Special Educational Needs', in Barton, L. and Oliver, M. (eds) *Disability Studies: Past, Present and Future*, Leeds: The Disability Press.

Barton, L. and Oliver, M. (eds) (1997) *Disability Studies: Past, Present and Future*, Leeds: The Disability Press.

An important document from the late 1990s setting out policy on 'special educational needs' is:

DfEE (1997) *Excellence for All Children: Meeting Special Educational Needs*, London: The Stationery Office.

An early critique of the policy of inclusion, from the USA, is:

Kauffman, J. and Hallahan, D. (eds) (1995) *The Illusion of Full Inclusion: A Comprehensive Critique of a Current Special Education Bandwagon*, Austin, TX: Pro-Ed.

Useful websites

http://inclusion.uwe.ac.uk/
http://www.inclusion.ac.uk/
http://www.parentsforinclusion.org/pihomepage.htm
http://www.scotland.gov.uk/library3/education/csen-04.asp
http://www.uni.edu/coe/inclusion/
Mary Warnock's criticism can be found at:
http://www.behaviour4learning.ac.uk/viewArticle.aspx?contentId = 10977
For a US perspective, try:
http://www.rushservices.com/Inclusion/homepage.htm

INFORMAL LEARNING

The central importance of learning which takes place outside of the school setting is now widely recognised, particularly with the widespread use of ICT in homes and other non-formal contexts.

It is useful to employ an ecological analogy in comparing informal, home learning with the more formal and statutory learning that occurs in schools. Ecology can be defined as the investigation of the total relations of an animal to both its organic and inorganic environment (based on the Greek words *oikos* meaning household or homestead, and *logos* meaning study). Kerawalla and Crook (2002) give an excellent discussion of 'domestic ecology' in contrast with that in school. They talk of the 'social envelope' (including social expectations and arrangements) and the systems of activity within which children learn in the two habitats. There is a huge contrast in the nature of the learning environment in the home compared with school: learning is linked to an adult at school (the teacher) compared with home learning which has little or no adult interference or engagement; social, paired, collaborative learning at school contrasts with the often isolated computer activity at home; the informal atmosphere of the home contrasts with the formal, more pressured environment at school.

So there are fundamental differences between learning in an institution which we know as a 'school' or 'college', and learning which does not take place under institutional constraints. Some of these contrasts are summarised in Table 3 (p116). Table 3 shows the differences in the ecologies of domestic and school learning, with some of the key features of learning with ICT in the middle column. It illustrates that home learning and the domestic ecology are far more akin and conducive to learning with ICT than school or classroom learning.

The importance of informal or home learning is certain to grow – indeed, many educators argue that it already has more impact on a child's or student's learning and development than does formal schooling.

Reference

Kerawalla, L. and Crook, C. (2002) 'Children's Computer Use at Home and at School: Context and Continuity', *British Educational Research Journal*, 28 (6): 751–71.

Useful websites

http://agelesslearner.com/intros/informal.html
http://www.infed.org/features/informal_learning.htm

INTELLIGENCE

There is no single (let alone simple) agreed definition of intelligence. A number of definitions have been proposed: 'general mental efficiency'

Table 3 Differences in the ecologies of domestic and school learning compared with learning using ICT

Classroom learning	Learning with ICT	Informal home learning
Conformity and order are central Learning is compulsory and collective	Personal empowerment is central Learning is individualised (usually)	Voluntary; personal, individual (often)
Keeping people, 'together', 'on track' On course, directed Staged, sequenced, paced learning	Exploring, having a free rein Going their own way Free access to information	Free range, undirected, haphazard, unstructured, not sequenced
Measurable learning outcomes; assessment-driven; extrinsically motivated	Free-ranging learning outcomes	Many unintended outcomes (outcomes more difficult to measure); not always assessment-driven or extrinsically motivated
Timetabled, 'forced' access Teacher control	Flexible access, when it suits them; learner or teacher control	Free access; learner (or parent) control
Clear boundaries and targets, e.g. times, deadlines, subject divisions	Unclear boundaries and targets	Few boundaries and limits; open-ended
Teacher-led, teacher-centred	Learner-led, learner-centred	Learner-centred
Teacher filtered, distilled, vetted	Unfiltered, not always vetted or censored	Often unfiltered or unvetted
Legislated for, e.g. by national curriculum or other statues	Not always governed by documents	Not legislated for

(Burt, 1949); 'a general reasoning capacity' (Kline, 1991); 'innate general cognitive ability' (Burt, 1955), but as yet, no one definition has been established, largely because the nature of 'intelligence' is disputed, and the processes underlying it are so complex and wide-ranging.

As well as the dispute about what intelligence is, there are several other recurring debates about intelligence that have already lasted for one century and may well continue for another. First, is intelligence one general ability or are there different specific 'intelligences'? Some theorists view 'intelligence' as dependent on a unitary and general underlying process (referred to as 'g' by Charles Spearman, 1927); 'g' is said to be the 'abstract reasoning power' which underlies many tests of intelligence. In contrast, others regard it as having multiple facets (Thurstone, 1938) or even support the existence of *multiple* and independent categories of 'intelligence' (Gardner, 1993).

Second, does intelligence come from nature or nurture? Is it determined by our genes or our environment? Is it inherited or acquired? The first half of the twentieth century was dominated by a belief in an innate general intelligence, thought to be fixed and measurable. This belief in innate ability continued until at least the 1960s with famous advocates such as Arthur Jensen. However, the innate interpretation has become less credible for two reasons:

- Because intelligence seems to change over time. This is sometimes called the Flynn Effect, after the psychologist of that name who found clear 'generational gains' in intelligence. Flynn (1994) showed that IQs have increased steadily since the 1930s, in one country as much as 18 points in a generation (a 30-year period). He and others have speculated that it may be due to factors such as improved diet from one generation to the next, longer compulsory schooling, the introduction of technology such as computers and a more stimulating world. This cannot be due to genetics as human genes have hardly changed in the last 100,000 years.

- Other studies have indicated that an individual's intelligence is influenced by more than a set of inherited abilities (it is not just 'in the blood'). There are a number of environmental factors which seem to influence a person's intelligence. On the positive side they include time spent in schooling, health, nutrition/diet, physical environment and parental support. One of the difficulties, however, has been in showing any cause and effect relationships between these variables and intelligence: partly, because they often cluster together, e.g. parental support for learning and a good diet; and partly because they interact with each other. On the other side of the coin, certain environmental factors, e.g. pollutants such as lead in the air; poor diet or food additives, have been linked with a lowering of intelligence.

The third debate is over intelligence testing: IQ tests do give a measure of a wide range of cognitive processes, but do they actually measure intelligence? IQ tests were developed on the basis of operationalism: that is, in order to understand 'intelligence' some measurement of individual differences in the process must be obtained. The intelligence quotient (IQ) is the ratio of a child's mental to chronological age and this is often compared to the scores of a comparable group of people: thus, IQ = mental age/chronological age × 100.

Among initial test attempts were those by Francis Galton (1869) and James Cattell (1890), both of which proved largely unsuccessful. In the twentieth century, a vast spectrum of IQ tests was developed, allegedly measuring an array of supposed intelligence-related cognitive processes, for example, spatial, verbal reasoning, perceptual and speed skills, and presented in differing formats: multiple choice, examiner-assisted, and so on. The Stanford–Binet tests are the best-known examples of measures of intelligence for verbal reasoning, quantitative reasoning, abstract/visual reasoning and short-term memory: collectively, they provide a composite score which is generally interpreted as an IQ score.

Although vastly improved from initial test attempts, IQ tests remain controversial and are often strongly criticised. There is some evidence to suggest that IQ tests are reliable (i.e. the results they yield reflect something other than a chance relationship) but high reliability does not show that IQ tests are actually measuring variance in intelligence, i.e. that they are valid. They may in fact be measuring an alternative stable trait that affects variance in IQ scores. Perhaps more significant evidence that IQ tests are valid (they measure what they claim to measure) is the high correlations between a range of IQ tests. IQ tests are diverse in their content and administration, yet at present it is difficult to find an IQ test that does not correlate with existing IQ tests.

Nevertheless, unconvinced critics say that the only thing that all IQ tests measure is the ability to do IQ tests. Thus a high test score confirms the possession of the cognitive ability to succeed in the test – but a low test score does not indicate the absence of ability or the labelling of a student as a 'low-ability' pupil.

Finally, the one debate about intelligence tests that has generated more pages of print (and often more heat than light) than any other is the alleged difference between groups in their 'intelligence'. Different groups have performed differently in tests of IQ that have been administered to them (rather than for them). Historically, groups have been divided into categories according to: ethnicity/race; social class; cultural divisions; peasant/professional; rural/urban; male/female. In the early twentieth century, controversial research used IQ tests in which 'blacks' obtained lower scores than 'whites'. This was used, by some commentators, to argue that blacks were less intelligent. Other research in the past has been used to identify 'feeble-minded people' and even gave fuel to the Eugenics movement in the early twentieth century, which argued for direct intervention and birth control in order to eradicate 'feeble-mindedness'. In England, following the 1944 Education Act, the 11-plus tests (which claimed to test intelligence) were used to underpin the tri-partite system of secondary schooling with its three types of pupil: grammar, secondary modern and technical.

Thus intelligence testing has been greeted with scepticism and even scorn from a variety of viewpoints. The main criticism concerns the apparent cultural bias in IQ tests. The majority were designed for Western industrial societies, to measure the cognitive abilities valued specifically in Western educational systems and general society. In addition, most are administered by and to Caucasians, with possible disregard for ethnic differences within modern Western societies. Differences in upbringing according to ethnicity seem to affect performance in IQ tests. For example, Hispanic children are said to expect adults to know the answer and are not encouraged to express their own views; while in African American homes the majority of parental questions directed at children from parents are real, rather than prompts. Such factors may adversely affect the performance of ethnic minority children on IQ tests. Thus, the design and structure of the test itself, not actual variation in 'general ability', may be to blame for alleged disparities in intelligence: in a test designed specifically for black people, they obtained an average score of 80/90, while Caucasians obtained a mean score of 50/60 (see Mackintosh, 1998, pp. 175–80, for an excellent discussion of this).

Another criticism of IQ tests is that they measure knowledge, richness of experience and width of vocabulary rather than 'intelligence' – and these are acquired through differential home background, social class and educational opportunity. Specific criticism has been levelled at measures of verbal ability which include vocabulary, general knowledge and verbal comprehension tests. A further criticism is that, at best, IQ tests measure only one or two facets of intelligence from a range of possibly eight **'multiple intelligences'** and ignore all the others such as musical, interpersonal or kinaesthetic.

Debates on intelligence and its connection with education and academic achievement seem set to continue. At the root of the debate is the issue that we started out with: the question of whether any test that measures 'intelligence' is dependent on how we define intelligence. Current thinking suggests that there is not one single entity, 'thing' or general ability (g) that 'intelligence' is, and indeed questions the existence of 'g'. So we can probably say that while tests certainly do not capture the measurement of g, they certainly do measure a wide range of cognitive processes that seem to be necessary for intelligent behaviour.

References and further reading

This list includes some of the classic literature on intelligence and an excellent summary at the end of the twentieth century by Mackintosh:

Burt, C. (1949) 'The Structure of the Mind', *British Journal of Educational Psychology*, 19: 176–99.

——(1955) 'The Evidence for the Concept of Intelligence', *British Journal of Educational Psychology*, 25: 158–77.

Flynn, J. (1994) 'IQ Gains over Time in Sternberg, R. J. (ed.) *The Encyclopaedia of Human Intelligence*, New York: Macmillan, pp. 617–23.

Gardner, H. (1993) *Frames of Mind* (second edition), London: Fontana.

Kline, P. (1991) *Intelligence: The Psychometric View*, London: Routledge.

Mackintosh, N. (1998) *IQ and Human Intelligence*, Oxford: Oxford University Press.

Spearman, C. (1927) *The Abilities of Man*, London: Macmillan.

Thurstone, L. (1938) *Primary Mental Abilities*, Chicago: University of Chicago Press.

Useful websites

There is a huge range of websites on intelligence though many seem to adopt one point of view or another. One exception is a useful, historical summary at
http://www.indiana.edu/~intell/

One of the papers by Arthur Jensen, linked to the Eugenics movement:
http://www.eugenics.net/papers/eb2.html

On alleged links between diet and intelligence:
http://www.beyondveg.com/billings-t/comp-anat/comp-anat-4a.shtml

For the humanist view:
http://www.progressivehumanism.com/intelligence.html

INTERNET

The use of the Internet as an educational tool is now widespread in schools, colleges, universities and (last but definitely not least) in homes. Wide area networks of computers will play an increasingly significant role in learning and teaching in the twenty-first century – the Internet is perhaps the most significant of these networks. It is a global system connecting computers on smaller networks, many of which are located in schools, universities and government as well as commercial companies. These Internet computers are now numbered in their millions and users in scores of millions. Both figures are increasing at an astonishing rate.

One of the most common ways of using the Internet is via the World Wide Web (WWW). This is a hypertext system which allows the user to access information on a very wide range of subjects. The information appears as pages of text, with graphics, sound and sometimes video too. The pages are linked to one another by hot links, and moving from page to page is easy even though the two pages may be on computers in different countries. There are a number of computers connected to the World Wide Web which run programs called *search engines*. These enable students to search for pages that contain a certain word (or words).

The value and potential of the Internet in teaching

There is a long list of features that the Internet provides for education, for example:

- sharing and exchanging information;
- communicating;
- accessing information;
- a local exchange of information on resources, e.g. for pooling;
- linking with industry;
- giving current information to pupils/students;
- improving study skills and search skills;
- giving pupils the excitement of on-line computer information;
- allowing collaboration: between pupil and pupil, school and school, teacher and teacher;
- downloading material;
- setting up a forum for debate and queries among teachers.

Words of warning

Most people agree that the Internet is *potentially* a powerful resource for education but as critical teachers we need to avoid being carried away by the hype that often surrounds it. It certainly has educational value in three areas: exchanging and sharing ideas and information, e.g. between teacher and teacher, pupil to pupil or a mixture of both; in enhancing and enabling communication, e.g. by e-mail; and third, in providing a source of information for learners and teachers on almost any topic from football to photosynthesis. The value of the first two uses for education is beyond doubt.

But use of the Internet as a vast source of information for schools and higher education is more problematic. Yes, there is a huge supply of data on every topic – but this is at once its potential and its downfall. How much of that information has been checked and edited, or even proofread? How accurate and reliable is the information? Who has written it and what were their motives? We should, quite rightly, treat all material on the Internet with a healthy scepticism, just as we would (or should) regard data in the national newspapers. This scepticism should be central to both the attitude of teachers and the message conveyed to learners.

Equally, the amount of information available is now so vast that it is extremely difficult for teachers to contain, or harness, it in order to meet the needs of a statutory curriculum. In my view, there are three major, inter-connected concerns for teachers in school: 'containing', vetting and drawing boundaries round material; similarly, structuring and guiding learners through material; and last but probably foremost, *curriculum relevance*. If learners are let loose on the Internet, where will it all end? What relevance will it have to the 'delivery' of a national curriculum which, in many countries, has become the classroom teacher's main driving force? (And who can blame them, given the external pressures?)

The Internet does have curriculum relevance – but the challenge for teachers is to 'map' Internet sources onto their own subject curriculum and then their schemes of work. There are additional factors which can pose problems for teachers at all levels:

- the front end/usability of many websites;
- the need for more teacher experience in using the Net – requirement for more teacher time for them to get to know it;
- the need for more time to share experiences among themselves, e.g. in producing a list of useful sites;

- access by students and teachers – will access be equal, especially as home use increases?;
- slowness of the system, i.e. time taken in gaining access to something valuable, especially images and video;
- urgent need for pupils (and teachers) to develop search skills, e.g. use of search engines; discrimination/evaluation of information;
- is more information necessarily a good thing?;
- security of the 'walled gardens': how secure are they?; there is a need for censorship – what will happen if pupils get access to obscene or pornographic material? Who will get the blame? (Probably the classroom teacher.)
- ownership/copyright of material (including pupils' material);
- the lack of vetting/refereeing/filtering of material before it goes on the Net;
- viruses that may be carried;
- plagiarism by pupils and students, quoting without attributing the source;
- accuracy of information;
- partiality of information;
- people's motives for putting material on the Net;
- the language level of much material and the text handling difficulties it presents;
- the 'haphazard'/uncontrolled learning which will take place if pupils are allowed free access;
- the cost, who will pay the phone bills?

The Internet has huge potential for enhancing teaching and learning – I have also listed a range of factors, problems and issues that a reflective teacher needs to be aware of in using the Internet in a school context. Some things are certain: the use of the Internet as an educational tool will grow and the technology for using it and accessing it will evolve rapidly – but the educational issues outlined above will resurface, whatever the technology in use.

Further reading

Cuban, L. (2001) *Oversold and Underused: Computers in the Classroom*, Cambridge, MA: Harvard University Press.

De Cicco, E., Farmer, M. and Hargrave, J. (1998) *Using the Internet in Secondary Schools*, London: Kogan Page.

DfEE (1997) *Connecting the Learning Society: National Grid for Learning*, London: Department for Education and Employment.

Grey, D. (2001) *The Internet in School*, London: Continuum.

Leask, M. (ed.) (2001) *Issues in Teaching using ICT*, London: Routledge-Falmer.

Russell, T. (2001) *Teaching and Using ICT in Secondary Schools*, London: David Fulton.

Wellington, J. (2001) 'Exploring the Secret Garden: The Growing Importance of ICT in the Home', *British Journal of Educational Technology*, 32(2): 233–44.

Useful websites

From a potential supply of over 38 million sites on Internet use in education, here are some of the most useful. The National Grid for Learning (NGfL) is said to 'provide a network of selected links to websites that offer high quality content and information':

http://www.ngfl.gov.uk/
    Children's and students' uses of the Internet in education:
http://nces.ed.gov/pubsearch/pubsinfo.asp?pubid = 2004014
http://www.ncrel.org/sdrs/areas/issues/methods/technlgy/te400.htm
http://www.iste.org/Content/NavigationMenu/Research/Reports/
    Research_on_Technology_in_Education_2000_/Internet/Research_on_
    Internet_Use_in_Education.htm
    Guidance on 'safe' use of the Internet:
http://safety.ngfl.gov.uk/?sec = 9&cat = 99&clear = y

KEY SKILLS

The idea behind 'key skills' (as they are now called) dates back to the 1970s when it was fashionable to talk of 'generic, transferable skills'. These become prominent in programmes such as the Youth Training Scheme of that era, which at one stage identified no less than 103 generic, transferable skills. The idea is based on the view that there are a number of core, transferable skills that we can use and apply to all sorts of areas in education and employment – skills such as problem solving, working with others and communication are often mentioned. It is worth noting that the idea of a set of skills being transferable and generic, whatever the context, runs contrary to many of the ideas of **'situated cognition'**.

Different lists and inventories of core skills have come from different sources such as employers' groups, work-based trainers and the National Curriculum Council. Thankfully, the lengthening lists of generic skills was trimmed down with the advent of 'core skills' later in the twentieth century – this was the set of skills that every school leaver and every trainee was said to need.

Much of the momentum for 'key skills' came from alleged concern from employers in the 1970s and 1980s that their young recruits did not have the general skills needed for employment (this actually originated in a famous speech in 1976 by the Labour Prime Minister of the time, James Callaghan, who grumbled that on 'his travels', employers were constantly complaining that young people did not have the 'necessary skills'). The emphasis on 'skills' continued with the re-naming of the department for Education as the DfES (Department for Education *and* Skills, as if they were two separate topics) and the creation of Learning and Skills Councils (LSCs).

Then, in 1996, the Dearing Review of post-16 education recommended that key skills should be included in both work-based and academic routes – they began to permeate higher education as well as the secondary curriculum and work-based training such as the Modern Apprenticeship. 'Key Skills' were introduced in 2000 in England, Wales and Northern Ireland, with similar Core Skills in Scotland. Currently, there are Key Skills qualifications from levels 1 to 4 in the three main key skills of: 'communication, application of number and information technology (IT)'. These are now available across all post-16 routes in England, Wales and Northern Ireland. Also available at these levels are the so-called 'wider key skills': 'working with others, improving own learning and performance, problem solving'.

For students and trainees working towards the Key Skill qualifications in Communication, Application of Number or IT, assessment requires both an internal (portfolio) and an external (test) component. For students and trainees working towards the wider Key Skill units in Working with Others, Improving Own Learning and Performance or Problem Solving, assessment is via an internal (portfolio) component alone.

The coming of core skills in the late twentieth century and then key skills was greeted with some cynicism by secondary school teachers and, to some extent, staff working in higher education. This can be attributed to several factors: first, their possession does not really carry the currency or kudos of traditional, academic qualifications; second, school teachers saw them as yet another initiative they had to respond to – some tried to ignore them in the hope that they might go away; the views of students on their value varied; the huge pressures of a subject-dominated National Curriculum, coupled with league tables showing only GCSE results, tended to downplay their importance for students and teachers; and the lack of strong evidence either that they had produced a generation of workers with more flexible and transferable skills or that they had helped to bridge the continuing gap between vocational and academic education (Green, 1998).

In addition, there has always been a tension in secondary schools about how key skills should be 'delivered'. The ideal would be to take a holistic approach by including and integrating them across all the subjects of the curriculum – thus every subject could include the main skills of communication, number and IT in this model. In reality, this rarely happened (in a similar way to other cross-curricular initiatives: see **citizenship**). The approach taken was to regard them as 'bolted on', a separate activity, i.e. something to be added rather than integrated. This meant that many students saw them purely as a requirement or 'yet another thing we have to do' – an attitude mirrored by some teachers. The introduction of external tests took the main key skills even further away from an integrated, cross-curricular model of delivery. Another effect was that the 'wider key skills' were seen as even lower in status than the main three and were often ignored.

In 2005, the UK Government were said to be promising a new focus on basic literacy and maths skills among secondary school students in England and this was said to be an acknowledgement that the push for key skills in 'Curriculum 2000' had failed. According to official figures in 2005, more than 360,000 people had taken Key Skills qualifications – mostly at the ages of 16 and 17 – but only 18 per cent of them did all three subjects (http://news.bbc.co.uk/1/hi/education/4285525.stm). The review of 14 to 19 learning in 2005 in England by Sir Mike Tomlinson concluded that new tests of 'functional' numeracy and literacy were needed, in addition to GCSE English and Maths. Research reported in 2005 by London University's Institute of Education suggested that one of the problems hindering the take-up of Key Skills is that universities do not value them. Although, in theory, they are worth points towards university entry, the entry requirements for 2004 published by the admissions service, UCAS, showed that only 49 per cent of institutions had at least one course where Key Skills tariff points were counted towards an offer of a place. The Institute of Education researchers also reported that many students loathed Key Skills.

The future of Key Skills in their present form remains uncertain; but the concept of, and the search for, a set of generic, transferable skills that everyone is said to need for either further education or for employment is unlikely to disappear.

Reference

Green, A. (1998) 'Core Skills, Key Skills and General Culture: In Search of the Common Foundation in Vocational Education', *Evaluation and Research in Education*, 12(1): 23–43.

Useful websites

The government view:
http://www.dfes.gov.uk/keyskills/
Statistics on Key Skills can be found at:
www.dfes.gov.uk/rsgateway/DB/SFR/s000459/index.shtml
For their role in post-16 education and training, see:
http://www.keyskillssupport.net/
The QCA's first report relating to Key Skills (entitled: *Review of Curriculum 2000 – Report on Phase One*) was published on 11 July 2001. The full text can be found on the QCA website at:
http://www.qca.org.uk/c2k/review2000_phase1.asp
The QCA *Final Report on the Curriculum 2000 Review*, presented to the Secretary of State in December 2001, can be found on the QCA website at:
http://www.qca.org.uk/pdf.asp?/nq/framework/c2k/c2k_phase2.pdf
The full text of the QCA *Key Skills Review* report can be found on the QCA website at:
http://www.qca.org.uk/pdf.asp?/nq/ks/key_skills_review01.pdf
The National Key Stage 3 strategy from the DfES has a number of pages on Key Skills at:
http://www.standards.dfes.gov.uk/keystage3/search/?mode = basic_search
&pagenumber = 1&d = m-ks3&search_string = key+skills

LEARNING SOCIETY

The learning society is a commonly discussed and widely heralded concept, but one that is rarely defined. At least three models of the learning society have been put forward. First, *credentialist/qualifications/skills growth*: learners build up 'capital' by acquiring skills and qualifications. They invest in themselves and the state invests in them, as 'human capital'. Credentials are seen as the key aim of a learning society; their growth will make individuals and states more economically competitive.

One of the problems with this approach to a learning society is that of 'qualification inflation': as more and more people gain higher and higher qualifications, the credentials that people do hold become devalued. In a sense, the value of a qualification depends on its scarcity, rather like gold. Another issue is that the drive for skills and credentials becomes an aim in itself and becomes disconnected from the actual skills and aptitudes needed for jobs in a changing society. Qualifications are simply a means of competing with others rather than contributing to a highly skilled workforce (Gleeson, 1990). This model also neglects some of the tacit knowledge, personal skills and characteristics, attitudes and behaviour seen as vital for the growing service sector (sometimes called 'soft skills'). Also, there is a danger of over-skilling and becoming over-qualified, e.g. graduates doing undemanding jobs.

Second, *social control*: in this model, the learning society has a hidden agenda; learning becomes a 'moral obligation and a social constraint' (Coffield, 2000, p. 488). We are all expected and required to become learners; it becomes a way of 'socialising' young people in an attempt to 'match' the needs of employers, a way of instilling the work ethic and making them more amenable, compliant and 'flexible' in response to employers' demands, such as short-term contracts and unpredictable hours, i.e. flexibility *for* the employer not the learner (Wellington, 1993).

Third, *social democratic*: learning is about participation, collaboration and dialogue – it is aimed towards social justice rather than economic competitiveness. This shifts the idea of capital towards social and **cultural capital** rather than individual capital and the focus moves towards networks and relationships – reduced inequality and more caring forms of social organisation. This somewhat utopian view is put forward by Coffield (2000) as one in which all citizens gain a high-quality education and continue to participate in education and training through their lives.

The term 'the learning society' is still widely used and politicians continue to delight in sprinkling it around in speeches; however, its meaning is far from clear and it tends to be used by individuals and groups with widely differing agendas but with the common assumption that it is a 'good thing'.

References and further reading

Coffield, F. (ed.) (2000) *Different Visions of a Learning Society*, Bristol: Policy Press.
DfEE (1998) *The Learning Age*, London: Department for Education and Employment.
Field, J. (2000) *Lifelong Learning and the New Educational Order*, Stoke-on-Trent: Trentham Books.
Gleeson, D. (1990) *Training and its Alternatives*, Buckingham: Open University Press.
Wellington, J. (1993) *The Work Related Curriculum*, London: Kogan Page.

Useful websites

http://www.elearningconference.org/
http://www.infed.org/lifelonglearning/b-lrnsoc.htm
http://www.staff.ncl.ac.uk/f.j.coffield/Default.htm

LEARNING STYLES

Although the concept of learning styles and preferences is not new, it has gained momentum in recent years for at least three reasons: (1) a government drive towards 'personalised learning'; (2) a growth in advocates of **brain-based learning** and educational consultants promoting it in certain education authorities and schools; and (3) the perpetual push for 'school improvement', particularly in so-called 'failing schools', which hope to use a focus on the learner and learning styles as a means of raising achievement.

The premise underlying learning styles is that different students have different preferences for the way they learn. For example, some prefer to learn visually, some by hearing (auditory learners) and some prefer to learn by doing, moving, touching or feeling (kinaesthetic). These three styles are usually abbreviated as VAK.

There are many other ways of labelling and categorising learning styles and preferences, dating back over 30 years. Some of these involve a 'learning styles analysis' (LSA) or a 'learning styles inventory' (LSI) which allegedly tells you what kind of learner you are by asking you to answer a range of questions (see websites below).

One of the early authors (Pask, 1975) argued that some people are 'serialist' learners (they learn by taking one element at a time) while others are 'holist', preferring to gain an overview first. Some learners prefer to move from specific, concrete examples to the abstract and general – others prefer to move the other way, from the abstraction and general rule or theory to the specific instances that come under it. Another LSI came from Kolb (1984) who talked about 'divergers' and 'convergers' on one dimension, and 'accommodators' versus 'assimilators' on another. Gregorc (1982) talked of different mind-sets or 'mindstyles' for learning: concrete sequential, abstract sequential, concrete random and abstract random. A later analysis came from Riding and Cheema (1991) who distinguished 'wholist' learners from analysts. The wholist uses a top-down approach and prefers to grasp the whole concept or idea first before concentrating on the specifics and the details. The 'analyst' prefers to process information in a step-by-step sequential manner, building up from the concrete instances to the general rule. Another dimension, or dichotomy, is between 'verbaliser' and 'imager'. The verbaliser is more comfortable in learning through the spoken or written word and finds it easy to assimilate verbal information. The imager prefers information and ideas presented in a diagrammatic or pictorial form and has difficulty in learning through words alone. Many of the ideas behind learning styles are related to Howard Gardner's (1993) appealing view that intelligence is multi-faceted and different people can be intelligent in different ways (see **multiple intelligences**). The ideas are also associated with movements such as brain gym, whole brain thinking, **thinking skills** and recognising diversity.

Most advocates of learning styles argue that students learn most effectively when they are taught in a style that best matches their preferred style of learning. The concept is in many ways very appealing but there are numerous questions that teachers could and should be asking about learning styles and learning inventories:

- What is the validity of the tests which indicate whether you happen to be one type of learner or another? With the proliferation of instruments and tests, how reliable are they? How well do the different tests correlate with each other?
- Can the same person have a different learning style according to mood, time of day, inclination, subject matter, and so on? Is it something a student is 'stuck with' over time?
- Is it dangerous to label learners as being of a certain type so that they carry that label and almost begin to believe in it, e.g. 'I'm a kinaesthetic learner'? Will these result in further labelling for 'under-achievers' and stereotyping of certain categories of student? For example, the vocational student as an 'activity-based learner'?
- Consequently, will it result in the kind of stereotyping and straitjacketing that education has been trying to avoid since the tripartism of 1944, with its 'three types of secondary pupil'?
- Does the learning style label become a self-fulfilling prophecy?
- What should teachers actually do about learning styles in the classroom, faced with a range of learning preferences and styles?
- Should learners and teachers play to the learner's strengths – or should they work on improving a learner's weaknesses? If learning how to learn is an aim of education, then surely each student should learn how to improve their learning in their least favoured style?

Radical approaches (such as Barbara Prashnig's: see website below) have introduced a wide range of physical and other environmental conditions into a classroom, e.g. different types of seating – some hard, some soft, with cushions or without; different types of lighting – brighter for some, dimmer for others, some fluorescent and some not; the use of music to enhance the holistic learners' progress, but quiet for others; different temperature levels; drinking water for those who want it; different groupings, with some students allowed to work on their own, others in peer groups.

More moderate approaches have seen teachers openly and helpfully introduce variety into their lesson planning (e.g. by using a VAK checklist) in order to recognise the variety of learning styles present in any one class, on any one day.

Recent years have seen the learning styles approach become both a bandwagon and an industry, with in-service training days, paid consultants, websites and books on the topic proliferating. As with the advent of brain-based learning and brain gym, it is interesting to wonder where this momentum came from. Some of the impetus came from a push from the Labour Government in 2004 onwards to make 'personalised learning' a key priority area and ministers claimed that a greater emphasis on learning styles could help to achieve this and encourage students to shape their own learning and education; but the movement was well under way before then and most of the key texts on it date back to the 1970s and the 1980s. In some ways it is welcome and admirable in that the learning styles movement shifts the focus onto the learner and the importance of diversity. But in other ways it needs to be closely watched so that it does not become a dogma underlying the 'raising standards' and 'school improvement' lobbies, nor a panacea for the problems of alleged 'under-achievement' or 'failing schools'.

References and further reading

Some of the early texts are:

Gardner, H. (1993) *Frames of Mind* (second edition), London: Fontana.

Gregorc, A. (1982) *An Adult's Guide to Styles*, Maynard, MA: Gabriel Systems.

Honey, P. and Mumford, A. (1982) *Manual of Learning Styles*, London: P. Honey.

Kolb, D. (1984) *Experiential Learning: Experience as the Source of Learning and Development*, Englewood Cliffs, NJ: Prentice-Hall.

Pask, G. (1975) *The Cybernetics of Human Learning and Performance*, London: Hutchinson.

Riding, R. and Cheema, I. (1991) 'Cognitive Style: An Overview and Integration', *Educational Psychology*, 11: 193–215.

More recently:
Riding, R. (2002) *School Learning and Cognitive Style*, London: David Fulton.

Useful websites

http://pss.uvm.edu/pss162/learning_styles.html#1
http://www.ldpride.net/learningstyles.MI.htm
To check for your own VAK tendencies, try:
http://www.chaminade.org/inspire/learnstl.htm
As an example of the types of the educational consultancy that has sprung up around the idea of learning styles, see Barbara Prashnig's 'Creative Learning company' at:
http://www.creativelearningcentre.com/default.asp
On 'personalised learning':
http://www.standards.dfes.gov.uk/personalisedlearning/
The National Key Stage 3 strategy for the DfES has several pages on learning styles and brain gym at:
http://www.standards.dfes.gov.uk/keystage3/search/?mode = basic_search
&pagenumber = 1&d = m-ks3&search_string = brain+gym

LEARNING THEORIES

What is learning?

Roughly speaking, *learning* occurs when experiences cause a relatively permanent change in someone's knowledge, attitude, belief, perception or behaviour. For example:

- We sometimes act differently as a result of something we have learnt.
- We may learn a new skill and be able to perform differently or do a new task.
- We may learn to see something in a new way or see things we never saw before.
- Our beliefs and attitudes may change as a result of a learning event or an experience.

These changes can occur as a result of formal, classroom-based learning, i.e. deliberate, intended learning. But change can also occur due to unintentional learning or it may result from 'informal learning', e.g. watching television, listening to peers. Learning may be for the better or for worse – it is not always predictable and intended.

There is no single, definitive theory of how learning occurs (and arguably there never will be). Instead, a range of 'theories of learning' can be drawn upon. There are many categories of learning theory but some of the major ones can be crudely classified as: developmental, socio-cultural, ecological and situated. There are also a few important '-isms' and some key names.

Behaviourism

This model of learning began in the early twentieth century and has had its fierce critics but it still resurfaces occasionally. The model held that the mind should be treated as a 'black box' – we should not attempt to uncover the hidden workings of the mind but instead study only directly observable events. These were called *stimulus* (the input) and *response* (the output). The bit in the middle – the mind – was to be treated as a black box. Some of the famous names connected to this '-ism' are Pavlov, John Watson and Skinner. Pavlov's dogs became famous because they salivated (response) when they heard a bell ring (stimulus). This occurred because they associated the dog trainer's bell with feeding time – by associating the bell with food they became *conditioned*. Watson conducted similar experiments with children, 'moulding' their behaviour by carefully controlling the stimulus and the response. If the correct response is rewarded in some way, the required behaviour can be *reinforced*. Reinforcers can include food and drink, praise, a new toy or a nice smile. Unwanted behaviour can be discouraged by punishment, though this is not as effective in shaping and moulding behaviour as the use of rewards. Their approach became known as 'operant conditioning' after the work of B. F. Skinner (1904–90). Behaviourism had a huge influence on child psychology and indeed on teacher training and teaching for some time. It continues to have an influence, both useful and less useful, in schools and classrooms.

One offshoot of behaviourism was social learning theory (Bandura, 1977). This built on the ideas of conditioning and reinforcement but added the importance of social learning, i.e. learning by observing and imitating others' behaviour. The idea of *modelling* is the key. By watching others in the classroom or at play and also receiving feedback on their own actions, children can develop good personal standards and a sense of 'self-efficacy' (on a negative note, they could also develop poor habits and standards, and lack self-esteem given the wrong learning environment or role models). The combination of behaviourism and social learning theory led to the idea of *behaviour modification*, which has been used in schools where students show 'challenging behaviour' (though this has not yet been tried with the teachers). This uses a combination of conditioning (including rewards) and modelling to reinforce desirable behaviour and eliminate less desirable responses.

Although behaviourism once dominated, it is certainly less 'fashionable' now, but still has a presence. Its main weakness is its disregard for the learner's feelings, wishes and mental processes. To their credit, the behaviourists stressed the importance of the environment in children's development but their critics would say that they took too narrow a view of the learning environment. To some extent this was rectified by ecological theory (see below).

Constructivism

Behaviourism studied external factors connected with learning and how they might be manipulated. The focus was on inputs and outcomes which are visible, observable and measurable, i.e. behaviours and actions. In direct contrast to behaviourism, constructivism focuses on the learner and the personal meanings they make based on their prior experience, knowledge and interests. Constructivist theory holds that prior knowledge is of primary importance. Rather than learners being empty vessels into which information can be poured, they come with a wealth of knowledge already organised. It is upon this knowledge structure that learners attach new information, thus creating new links to their pre-existing knowledge. To learn meaningfully, a person must integrate new knowledge into his or her conceptual structure.

One of the early constructivists was the American educationalist, John Dewey, known for his stress on *experiential learning*. Dewey argued that experience is a key factor in learning: 'The more a teacher is aware of the past experiences of students ... the better will he understand the forces at work that need to be directed and utilised for the formation of reflective habits' (Dewey, 1933, p. 36). Dewey also believed that the role of education was to foster and encourage a love of learning. He saw learning in its broadest sense as a lifelong individual and social process.

George Hein (1992, 1998) proposed a set of nine learning principles that emerged from constructivist thought:

- learning is an active process of constructing meaning from sensory input;
- as they learn, people learn about the process of learning, as well as content;

- learning happens in the mind;
- language and learning are inextricably linked;
- learning is a social activity and happens with others;
- learning is contextual, in that we learn in relation to what we already know, our beliefs and our prejudices;
- previous knowledge is a prerequisite to learning;
- learning happens over long periods of time, through repeated exposure and thought;
- motivation is essential for learning.

Cognitive development theory and Jean Piaget

One of the people most commonly associated with constructivism is Jean Piaget (1896–1980). Piaget believed that knowledge is constructed by a child, rather than imposed by conditioning and reenforcement. He suggested that children progress through levels or stages of development. These go from the sensorimotor through the concrete operational to the formal operational stages:

1 *Sensorimotor: birth to 2 years*: infants think and learn by acting: touching, grabbing, sucking, feeling, picking up and dropping.
2 *Pre-operational: 2–7 years*: children begin to use symbols to represent their sensorimotor discoveries; language develops and pretend-play; but thinking is not yet logical.
3 *Concrete operational: 7–11 years*: reasoning becomes more logical; children can begin to classify and organise things into groups; but thinking is still not abstract.
4 *Formal operational: 11 years and above*: abstract thought begins and children can reason with symbols that do not refer to concrete objects; they can think about a range of outcomes, e.g. to solve a problem.

Some pupils, although chronologically beyond the transition age (of around 11 years old) from concrete to formal operations, may still be operating at the concrete level of classification and ordering (Child, 1977, p. 125). Although there have been criticisms about Piaget's work relating to development, research methods and language (Ausubel *et al.*, 1978, pp. 230–1; Child, 1977, p. 128; Scaife, 2000, p. 66), it is worth noting the comment from Adey (1992, p. 137) that only about 30 per cent of 16 year olds show the ability to use higher-level thinking associated with levels 6/7 of the National Curriculum.

Piaget's ideas on development are based on the biological idea of *adaptation*. Just as animals and their bodies adapt to their environment, so the learner's mind adapts its structures to cope with the world of observations and experiences. They adapt by a dual process of *accommodation* and *assimilation*:

- Accommodation = the ability of the mind to modify itself in the light of new experiences.
- Assimilation = the mind's ability to take in experiences and information.

The processes of accommodation and assimilation allow the learner to keep equilibrium, i.e. a balance between internal mental structures (schemata) and new information and experiences in the world. Thus, for Piaget, cognitive development involves the assimilation of new experiences into a child's cognitive structure; if these are in conflict with existing structures, there is a need to change so that the mind's 'schemata' (structures) can accommodate the new experiences (Scaife, 2000, p. 65). This kind of 'cognitive conflict' can result in meaningful learning and *cognitive conflict* has been said to be a useful aid to learning in the classroom. However, Adey (1992, p. 139) comments that not everything that a pupil finds surprising or inexplicable will serve the potentially useful role of cognitive conflict, adding that: 'probably the majority of surprising experiences are shrugged off as "inexplicable" or uninteresting'.

Piaget has been criticised for basing his ideas partly on work with his own three children and generalising from them; and for implying that stages of development are somehow fixed, proceed stepwise in jumps and are age related; and finally for underestimating the role of training and teaching rather than learning by discovery. But many of the criticisms levelled at his work are unfair and no-one can deny his huge influence on learning theory and indeed on classroom practice, especially in subjects such as mathematics and science which follow a 'vertical', hierarchical structure (see **cognitive acceleration**).

Jerome Bruner and cognitive growth

Bruner's work relates to that of Piaget in that both view learning as an active process in which students construct new ideas or concepts based on their current knowledge. However, from the 1960s, Bruner developed his own models of cognitive growth. His approach, in contrast to Piaget, emphasised environmental, social, cultural and experiential factors, following the influence of thinkers such as Lev Vygotsky. 'How one conceives of education, we have finally come to recognize, is a function of how one conceives of the culture and its aims, professed and otherwise' (Bruner, 1996, pp. ix–x).

Bruner suggested three main stages of thinking which relate in some ways to Piaget's levels of development:

1 The stage of *enactive representation*: this occurs in the early years when children represent the world in terms of personal action. In this stage, young children rely extensively upon enactive modes to learn, i.e. learning through their own actions. As a child learns to roll over, crawl, sit up or walk, they are learning through these actions. While this mode is present in people of all ages, it is more dominant when a person is young.

2 *Iconic representation* is the stage of development when we learn to represent the world in terms of concrete mental images. Iconic representation normally dominates during the stage of childhood following the enactive phase. Children learn to understand what pictures and diagrams are and how to do arithmetic using numbers rather than just counting objects.

3 *Symbolic representation* is the final stage of development in which children represent their world in symbols. This includes language and theoretical systems, such as mathematical symbols. Later, often around adolescence, the symbolic mode of learning becomes most dominant. Students can understand and work with concepts that are abstract and are represented in symbolic form.

The three stages (enactive, iconic, symbolic) emerge in a developmental sequence. Part of a learner's development involves becoming more skilled in swapping between each mode. An example of this could be a class or peer group discussion (symbolic mode) of what the students had learned from a practical activity such as a science experiment (iconic mode). The use of graphs and charts to represent their practical work would involve the iconic mode. An implication of Bruner's developmental theories is that children should be provided with activities, resources and tools (such as ICT) that are carefully matched to the right mode and will therefore help to enhance their developing cognitive abilities.

Bruner, unlike Piaget, did not argue for the age dependency of the stages of development, but stressed the role of teaching (instruction) and environment in the development of the learner. One of Piaget's key ideas was that of 'readiness to learn', whereas Bruner's emphasis was on making the material to be learned ready for the learner. His best-known idea on teaching (instruction, as he called it) is that any subject can be taught in some intellectually honest form to any child, regardless of their maturity level or stage of development (see *The Process of Education*, 1960).

In some ways he argued against the idea of 'readiness for learning' by suggesting that schools waste time by postponing the teaching of important areas because they are deemed 'too difficult'.

He also stressed the importance of *structure* in learning and how it is a vital element in effective teaching:

> The teaching and learning of structure, rather than simply the mastery of facts and techniques, is at the centre of the classic problem of transfer ... If earlier learning is to render later learning easier, it must do so by providing a general picture in terms of which the relations between things encountered earlier and later are made as clear as possible.
>
> (Bruner, 1960, p. 12)

This notion underpins the idea of the **spiral curriculum**. This is the view that a curriculum, as it develops, should revisit the key basic ideas repeatedly, building upon them at each stage and gradually deepening a student's understanding. Finally, Bruner emphasised the role of the teacher in deciding on the most effective sequence in which to present material and in pacing it appropriately.

Socio-cultural theory and Lev Vygotsky

A similar kind of theory can be called socio-cultural theory. This came from the work of the Russian Lev Vygotsky, who first proposed that learning was a social process. In a socio-cultural model, learning is shaped by the social context (e.g. the family, the classroom the child is in), the learner's culture, and the 'tools' used by the teacher in the classroom situation. Vygotsky agreed with Piaget that learners are active, constructive beings. But Vygotsky rightly showed the key role of teachers, classroom assistants and a child's peers in learning. He showed that learning leads to development as much as development leads to learning.

Vygotsky stressed the importance of the use of language in the classroom. He emphasised how children's discussion and talk in the classroom should go along with practical activity. Peers can be a valuable resource in the classroom, at any age, if pupils work together, discuss ideas and support each other.

One of Vygotsky's most memorable (for teachers at least) contributions has been to highlight the importance of teachers and other adults in learning. The development and maturation of a child's higher-level thinking come about as a result of co-operation with a teacher. He came up with the idea of a **zone of proximal development** (the ZPD). This is the 'learning zone' that teachers should aim at with their pupils – it is the zone between the pupil's actual level of development and the level they could reach with the right teaching, help and support (sometimes called 'scaffolding'). The ZPD is the region between 'where they are at' (actual level) and where they could be (the potential level).

Communities of learners and learning communities

One of the main criticisms levelled at theories of learning which focus on individuals and their development is that they tend to separate the learner from the learning environment, and focus on the learner in isolation. Psychologists at the end of the twentieth century began to focus increasingly on the environment and on learning communities. Learners cannot be separated from the environment and studied in isolation – they need to be considered *in situ*. We all experience learning in a context, in a particular situation. People often learn within a **community of practice**, e.g. as apprentices. They learn by participating in the community, at first, on the margins or peripherally; then gradually becoming more immersed and more central in the community. This could apply as much to scientists, engineers, doctors and solicitors as it could to musicians, plumbers, carpenters, scuba divers or footballers. The early phase has been christened 'legitimate peripheral participation' (Lave and Wenger, 1991).

Ecological systems theory

This view of the learner as inseparable from her or his environment has also led to the growth of ecological ways and ecological metaphors for considering learners as part of an ecosystem or a habitat. Learning theorists (Bronfenbrenner, 2004) divide the environment into various levels like onion skins or nested structures. The learner's immediate environment, usually the family, is called the *microsystem*. The interactions, between learner and parent or carer and vice versa, affect development hugely. A caring supportive, encouraging, praising environment will be in direct contrast to a microsystem characterised by hostility, inconsistent discipline, discouragement and punishment. The *mesosystem* is the layer where connections between home, school, and the locality take place. If these connections are good, e.g.

between home and school, then learning is enhanced. The third layer of the onion is the *exosystem*: the layer that does not 'contain' the child or student but still affects them. This could be the parents' working lives and their arrangements, e.g. for sick leave or holidays. It could be the parents' social networks (see **cultural capital**) or their ties and connections in the community. Finally, the *macrosystem*: this is the context made up of the cultural values, the laws, the resources, and customs of the country they live in. The country's wealth and institutions, e.g. schools, child care centres, libraries, will have a major impact on the student's experience and the other three levels of the eco-system. The overall system is not fixed but changes over time at all four levels, e.g. if a child has a new sibling; if the parents separate; if a school improves or gets worse; if a country becomes more or less affluent; if the government changes. The child or student is also an active agent: children are both products and producers in the learning environment – just as animals, plants, predators and prey all play a part in changing a natural ecosystem. The value of this theory is that it stresses the equal importance played by innate qualities and environment in learning – a balance between nature and nurture.

Conclusion

There are, and have been, many theories of learning and how it occurs. No one theory can be said to be 'true' or definitive. Currently, one of the features that all models, metaphors and theories used to describe the process of learning have in common is the belief that people 'make' knowledge. They are best viewed as 'active constructors' as opposed to 'hunter–gatherers' – the mind is best seen as something which 'assimilates and accommodates', as opposed to having things copied onto it like a blank slate or a hard disk drive.

References and further reading

Adey, P. (1992) 'The CASE Results: Implications for Science Teaching', *International Journal of Science Education*, 14(2): 137–46.

Ausubel, D. P., Novak, J. D. and Hanesian, H. (1978) *Educational Psychology: A Cognitive View*, 2nd edn, New York: Holt, Rinehart and Winston.

Bandura, A. (1977) *Social Learning Theory*, Englewood Cliffs, NJ: Prentice-Hall.

Bronfenbrenner, U. (2004) *Making Human Beings Human: Bioecological Perspectives on Human Development*, London: Sage.

Bruner, J. S. (1960) *The Process of Education*, Cambridge, MA: Harvard University Press.

——(1966) *Toward a Theory of Instruction*, Cambridge, MA: Belknap Press.

——(1996) *The Culture of Education*, Cambridge, MA: Harvard University Press.

Child, D. (1977) *Psychology and the Teacher*, 2nd edn, London: Holt, Rinehart and Winston.

Daniels, H. (2001) *Vygotsky and Pedagogy*, London: RoutledgeFalmer.

Dewey, J. (1933) *How We Think: A Re-statement of the Relation of Reflective Thinking to Educational Practice*, Boston: D. C. Heath.

——(1938) *Experience and Education*, New York: Kappa Delta Pi.

Dierking, L. (1989) 'Learning Theory and Learning Styles: An Overview', *Journal of Museum Education*, 14(1): 4–6.

Hein, G. (1992) Constructivist Learning Theory, *Developing Museum Exhibitions for Lifelong Learning*, London: The Stationery Office, pp. 30–4.

——(1998) *Learning in the Museum*, London: Routledge.

Lave, J. and Wenger, A. (1991) *Situated Learning: Legitimate Peripheral Participation*, Cambridge: Cambridge University Press.

Scaife, J. (2000) 'Learning in Science', in Wellington, J. (ed.) *Teaching and Learning Secondary Science*, London: Routledge, pp. 61–108.

Vygotsky, L. S. (1978) *Mind in Society*, Cambridge, MA: Harvard University Press.

——(1986) *Thought and Language*, Cambridge, MA: MIT Press.

Wenger, E. (1998) *Communities of Practice: Learning, Meaning and Identity*, Cambridge: Cambridge University Press.

Wood, D. (1988) *How Children Think and Learn*, Oxford: Blackwell.

Useful websites

On behaviourism:

http://www.forerunner.com/forerunner/X0497_DeMar—Behaviorism. html

http://www.funderstanding.com/behaviorism.cfm

On constructivism:

http://www.cdli.ca/~elmurphy/emurphy/cle.html

http://www.funderstanding.com/constructivism.cfm

On Vygotsky:

http://www.marxists.org/archive/vygotsky/

On Piaget:

http://www.dmu.ac.uk/~jamesa/learning/piaget.htm

On Bruner:

http://spearfish.k12.sd.us/west/master/JewZA/bruner.html

http://www.infed.org/thinkers/bruner.htm (Smith, M. K., 2002, 'Jerome S. Bruner and the process of education', *The Encyclopaedia of Informal Education*)

On Bronfenbrenner and ecological theories of learning:

http://www.psy.pdx.edu/PsiCafe/KeyTheorists/Bronfenbrenner.htm

MASTERY LEARNING

Mastery learning is based on the idea that all pupils can learn (or 'master') a topic or a subject provided that it is presented in the right way and the pupil is given enough time and feedback. It relates back to some of the ideas of *behaviourist psychology* (see **learning theories**) and programmed learning from the 1960s. It is often said to be based on Benjamin Bloom's Learning for Mastery model (see references below). This idea experiences a revival from time to time, especially when there is a drive for 'personalised' or individualised learning or for the attainment of 'lower achievers' in schools to be raised.

Mastery learning applies best to a traditional content-focused curriculum and sequential subjects such as mathematics, physics and language learning although some of its advocates claim that it can be applied to 'horizontal' subjects such as history. The topic area to be learned has to be broken down into clear and well-defined learning objectives and then organised into smaller, sequentially organised chunks. This requires considerable effort by the teacher, software producer or textbook writer – but it is said that by doing this breaking down and sequencing of a topic, teachers become more familiar with it and better prepared to teach it.

The teacher, software producer or textbook writer must also provide frequent and specific feedback by using diagnostic and formative tests, as well as regularly correcting mistakes students make along their learning route. Pupils have to demonstrate mastery of each 'chunk' of learning before they can proceed to the next step.

To teach using a mastery learning approach, a teacher must do the following:

1 Break a course or a topic down into units of instruction or 'chunks', in a logical sequence, e.g. x has to be learnt before y can make sense.
2 Identify and state clearly the learning objectives for each unit.
3 Produce diagnostic tests before each unit is started.
4 Require students to demonstrate mastery of the objectives for each unit before moving on to the next one.
5 Give every student time to demonstrate their mastery of objectives.
6 Not allow students to proceed to a new chunk or unit before the previous one is 'mastered'.

Thus every pupil can work at their own pace if a course or programme is individualised, but advocates of mastery learning claim that it can also be accomplished with whole classes.

Its supporters claim that mastery learning can break the cycle of failure for certain pupils, such as 'minority and disadvantaged students'. Its *disadvantages* are that:

- Not all students will progress at the same pace and in a whole class situation this requires students who have demonstrated mastery to wait for those who have not.
- It requires considerable teacher preparation to provide a variety of materials for teaching and a large number of assessments.
- Some critics have also said that if only 'objective' tests are used, e.g. multiple-choice tests, this can lead to memorising and learning specifics rather than the higher levels of learning in **Bloom's taxonomy**.

Despite its critics, the idea of mastery learning was in some ways very positive since its starting point was the view that all children have the potential to learn, as long as they are provided with the suitable learning conditions and enough time in the classroom. It resulted in a radical shift in responsibility for teachers by shifting the blame for a student's failure on the means of instruction, not a lack of ability from the student (Bloom, 1981). As a model of learning and teaching it has been superseded by ideas such as **constructivism** (learners construct their own knowledge), but it is still of interest in the twenty-first century and some of its basic tenets do resurface from time to time.

References and further reading

Block, J. H. (1971) *Mastery Learning: Theory and Practice*, New York: Holt, Rinehart and Winston.

Block, J. H., Efthim, H. E. and Burns, R. B. (1989) *Building Effective Mastery Learning Schools*, New York: Longman.

Bloom, B. S. (1981) *All Our Children Learning*, New York: McGraw-Hill.

Carroll, J. B. (1963) 'A Model of School Learning', *Teachers College Record*, 64: 723–33.

Gagne, R. (1977) *The Conditions of Learning*, 3rd edn, New York: Holt, Rinehart and Winston.

Useful websites

http://allen.warren.net/ml.htm
http://a.web.umkc.edu/aitkenj/masterylearning.html
http://www.funderstanding.com/mastery_learning.cfm
http://xnet.rrc.mb.ca/glenh/mastery_learning.htm

MEANINGFUL LEARNING

Meaningful learning is sometimes called 'engaged learning'. What exactly is meaningful learning? According to Ausubel (1968, p. 337), 'If I had to reduce all educational psychology to just a single principle, I would say this: find out what the learner already knows and teach him (or her) accordingly.' This is often said to be the fundamental principle of meaningful learning: learning can only be meaningful if it builds on, and ties into, what the learner already knows. Otherwise it is disconnected and lacks meaning for the individual as, for example, rote learning. Meaningful learning is information that ties into previously learned materials and is immediately useful for the learner.

One of the key ideas underpinning meaningful learning is the notion of *advance organisers* (again from Ausubel, 1968). These are general statements that teachers make in advance about the new materials about to be learned. Their purpose is to relate new material to what the students already know (linking the familiar with the unfamiliar). An advance organiser in a lesson is often the brief introduction that a teacher gives about the new material to be covered; it usually consists of a few general ideas that will help students to organise the specific material about to follow. In this way, the new material can be 'assimilated' (see **learning theories**) into existing knowledge structures or schemata. The advance organiser is a kind of preview, designed to pre-activate prior knowledge and schemata, to make pupils ready and *receptive* to new learning. In short, they help students to learn new material because they provide a context for it.

Ausubel also coined the terms *receptive learning* and *expository teaching*; these define the expository teacher's role as selecting what is to be learned, structuring the proper learning environment, using materials appropriate to the students' levels and presenting them in an organised manner. The three phases of receptive learning involve: (1) the presentation of an advance organiser; (2) presentation of learning tasks/materials; and (3) tying information to existing information via questions, feedback, and class discussion.

Several strategies for teachers, in addition to using advance organisers, have been suggested for achieving meaningful learning:

1 eliciting or 'diagnosing' the learner's prior knowledge, skill or understanding;
2 taking students' prior knowledge into account in planning lessons and during the teaching situation;
3 scaffolding.

Ausubel's guidelines are said to be fundamental to a constructivist approach to learning and teaching (see **constructivism**).

Reference

Ausubel, D. (1968) *Educational Psychology: A Cognitive View,* New York: Holt, Rinehart and Winston.

Useful websites

http://www.ncrel.org/sdrs/areas/issues/students/earlycld/ea1lk1.htm
http://www.ncrel.org/sdrs/engaged.htm
http://www.projecttime.org/about/meaningfulLearning.html

METACOGNITION

The Greek word 'meta' has several senses but is often used to mean 'after' or 'behind'. In English usage it also seems to have acquired the sense of 'being above' as in 'metaphysics'(above or beyond physics) or 'metaphor' (literally meaning 'carrying after', carrying across or bridging of meaning). Thus, metacognition can be seen as the activity of looking down and reflecting on cognition – being aware of, thinking about and knowing about one's own thinking: thinking about thinking. One of the prominent 1970s' authors on this area wrote:

> Metacognition refers to one's knowledge concerning one's own cognitive processes and products or anything related to them. For example, I am engaging in metacognition if I notice that I am having more trouble learning A than B ... if I sense that I had better make a note of D before I forget it.
>
> (Flavell, 1976, p. 232)

Another author used the metaphor of 'coach' or 'manager' of a person's learning to explain metacognition (Schoenfeld, 1985).

It is often argued that metacognition can enhance a person's learning. By thinking about how we think and reflecting on how we learn, the process of learning can itself be enhanced.

Sceptics may regard 'metacognition' as a 'new fangled label for the old fashioned concept of "reflection"' (Smith, 1994, p. 22) but my own view is that it is a useful conceptual vehicle for linking several ideas. Thus, in some ways the concept is linked with constructivism: the view that we construct knowledge and understanding for ourselves as opposed to, say, having it 'transmitted' to us in some way (what Paulo Freire called the 'banking theory' of learning) (see **critical pedagogy** and **constructivism**). The banking model views 'knowing things' as a product of external influences and of adults communicating their knowledge like some sort of transmitted substance. An emphasis on metacognition stresses the importance of learners reflecting on their own learning and thinking in order to enhance learning and also (it is argued) to enable it to be transferred to, and applied in, other situations and contexts. In this way, for example, generic skills and strategies such as 'problem solving' can be developed rather than cognition being situated solely in one context (see **situated cognition** and **transfer of learning**). Thus, connections between classroom experiences and the 'outside world' can be improved through metacognitive links.

How is metacognition relevant to formal education and can it be taught? There is a growing body of belief (see websites below for sources) that if learners learn how to study and how to learn there will be a dramatic improvement in achievement. Programmes designed to enhance metacognitive skills have filtered down from higher and tertiary education to secondary and primary education. Somewhat ironically, direct instruction is sometimes given in how to study and how to learn. One author identified a range of strategies for studying and learning that appear to be effective in the classroom and therefore should be explicitly taught. Learners should be able to do the following:

- monitor their own existing knowledge, i.e. be aware of what they know already;
- know effective ways of recalling previously learnt knowledge ('metamemory' as it has been called);
- know which strategies are, and are not, effective for their own learning and be able to utilise those which are;
- plan an approach to a learning task which is likely to be successful;
- become aware of their own learning and memory capabilities and be realistic about which learning tasks they can succeed in.

(adapted from Ormrod, 1995)

There are now strong arguments for the value of improving metacognition in formal education/schooling. In the so-called 'information rich age' it can be argued that it is more important to learn how to learn and to be able to think about and manage one's own learning, than to retain large amounts of factual knowledge or information. The nineteenth-century character in Dickens, Gradgrind, who pleaded for teachers to 'Give them facts, facts, facts', has his twenty-first-century counterpart in those who argue for metacognition and information literacy.

References and further reading

Brown, A. L. (1978) 'Knowing When, Where and How to Remember: A Problem of Metacognition', in Glaser, R. (ed.) *Advances in Instructional Psychology,* vol. 1, Hillsdale, NJ: Lawrence Erlbaum.

Flavell, J. (1976) 'Metacognitive Aspects of Problem Solving', in Resnick, L. (ed.) *The Nature of Intelligence,* Hillsdale, NJ: Lawrence Erlbaum.

Hacker, D., Dunlosky, J. and Graesser, A. (eds) (1998) *Metacognition in Educational Theory and Practice,* London: Lawrence Erlbaum.

Mason, L. (1994) 'Analogy, Metaconceptual Awareness and Conceptual Change: A Classroom Study', *Educational Studies,* 20(2): 267–91.

Ormrod, J. E. (1995) *Human Learning,* London: Prentice-Hall.

Schoenfeld, A. H. (1985) 'Metacognitive and Epistemological Issues in Mathematical Understanding', in Silver, E. A. (ed.) *Teaching and Learning Mathematical Problem Solving: Multiple Research Perspectives,* Hillsdale, NJ: Lawrence Erlbaum.

Smith, F. (1994) *Understanding Reading,* 5th edn, Hillsdale, NJ: Lawrence Erlbaum.

Vygotsky, L. S. (1978) *Mind in Society: The Development of Higher Psychological Processes,* Cambridge, MA: Harvard University Press.

Useful websites

http://tip.psychology.org/meta.html
http://www.gse.buffalo.edu/fas/shuell/cep564/Metacog.htm
http://www.ioe.ac.uk/cdl/CHAT/chatmeta1.htm
http://www.ioe.ac.uk/cdl/CHAT/chatmeta2.htm

MOTIVATION

Motivation is now widely seen as the key to learning – the affective domain of **Bloom's taxonomy** is considered to be as important to successful schooling as the cognitive domain. What is motivation? The term is usually associated with words such as desire, enthusiasm, ambition, interest, commitment, inspiration, drive and 'hunger'. In psychological terms, motivation is usually defined as some sort of internal state or condition which serves to activate, arouse, energise or direct behaviour and to give it impetus, direction and focus.

Motivation is central to learning because its presence can lead to persistence, enthusiasm, commitment, perseverance and risk-taking by the pupil or student. Lack of motivation can lead to – and be fuelled by – fear of failure, low self-esteem and low self-expectations, creating a vicious downward circle.

Several theories relating to motivation are extremely valuable in considering learning and teaching, and have important practical implications. One of the early theorists on motivation was Abraham Maslow (1943) who put forward a *hierarchy of* needs that humans wish to, and are driven to, satisfy:

1 Physiological needs, e.g. hunger, thirst.
2 Security.
3 Social needs, e.g. to mix and interact with others; to have attention.
4 Esteem.
5 Self-actualisation.

Physiological needs are the most basic and Maslow placed these at the bottom of a pyramid, with the higher, less basic needs at the top (see Figure 6).

Maslow argued that a person needs to satisfy or be content with a need lower in the hierarchy (nearer the base of the pyramid) before higher-level needs can be satisfied. Critics have said that the levels should not be seen as linear, since some individuals could be seen as

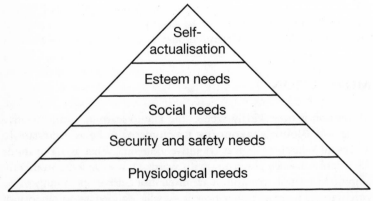

Figure 6 Maslow's hierarchy of needs

aiming to satisfy several needs at once. But the hierarchy still has important classroom implications. A student is unlikely to learn if he or she is hungry, tired, thirsty, sick or insecure. These needs may have to be satisfied if the student is to have success in learning and reach Maslow's higher levels, i.e. self-esteem and self-actualisation.

A second area of thinking on motivation has been called *attribution theory* (usually connected with Weiner, 1980, 1992). All students attribute certain characteristics to themselves to explain their success or failure. An unmotivated student, with low self-esteem, will blame his lack of success on his lack of 'ability', which he sees as fixed and unalterable (perhaps something they were born with, i.e. innate). When success does occur, he attributes this to luck or other factors outside his control, rather than his own effort and ability. In contrast, a highly motivated student attributes any success she has to her own ability and effort – she has confidence in her own ability and in the importance of making an effort to achieve success. Success or failure is not put down to external, uncontrollable factors such as luck or a tough examination. This view of oneself has been called 'self-efficacy' (Bandura, 1992): the belief in ourselves that we can alter our own future, we can control and influence our own learning and achievement. This contrasts with so-called 'learned helplessness': the feeling that our lack of achievement is outside our control and we cannot affect it by our own actions. Success is down to luck; failure is due to 'low ability'. This leads the learner to avoid attempting challenging tasks and not to take risks, while those with positive beliefs about their own characteristics and abilities will attempt a challenge and take risks.

The contrast between students with positive views of their own self-efficacy and students who learn 'helplessness' is related to the importance of expectations: both teacher expectations and pupil expectations. Pupils with high aspirations and high expectations may often achieve them, given the right conditions; if teachers have high expectations of pupils, this can lead to higher achievement. Low expectations held by teachers for their pupils, and by pupils of themselves, may lead to a downward spiral of achievement. The connection between expectation and achievement is usually described as 'self-fulfilling prophecy': if teachers predict that a child will do badly and somehow 'expect' it, this seems to have an effect on both the teacher and the pupil and the prophecy tends to come true. The effect of expectations can be seen in gender differences in education: girls are said to have higher expectations of themselves in 'feminine' areas such as art, writing, reading and literature; boys are said to have greater expectations in 'masculine' areas such as mathematics, technology, science and mechanical skills (Berk, 2003, p. 544). These expectations affect both subject choice in secondary schools and achievement.

Another vitally important distinction for the classroom is between *intrinsic and extrinsic motivation*. Intrinsic motivation comes from the learner's own interest, curiosity, personal satisfaction, and feelings of achievement, desire and need. Extrinsic motivation comes from rewards, external incentives, 'arm-twisters' and perhaps even avoidance of punishment. (This aspect of motivation is often associated with behaviourist psychology with its emphasis on using rewards, conditioning and punishment to 'shape' and determine behaviour; see **learning theories**.)

There is some debate on the relative importance of intrinsic and extrinsic motivation in schools. Clearly, the ideal position is that human learning (as opposed to the behaviourists' rats) is for its own sake – it is an end in itself as opposed to a 'means to an end' such as avoiding punishment or receiving an award. It has been argued that intrinsic motivation is much stronger and longer-lasting, leading ultimately to the highest levels of achievement. This may well be true. But the use of extrinsic motivation is not to be scoffed at – it can lead on to intrinsic motivation and it does not exclude it, i.e. the two can exist side by side. Payment for a job or a task does not preclude intrinsic enjoyment, fulfilment or satisfaction from it – witness the professional golfer or the successful doctor. In schools, extrinsic motivation provided by merit points, applause, praise, stickers or prizes for effort can have an important effect on pupils' self-esteem and thence achievement. It may be the precursor for intrinsic motivation and it can exist side by side with it. Praise, particularly, is recognised by classroom teachers as vitally important to students of any age and at any level.

To sum up, the practical implications of theories of motivation are as follows:

- The **affective domain** (motivation, enthusiasm, feeling) is as important as the cognitive domain (skill, knowledge, understanding) in successful learning.
- Intrinsic motivation for learning is the ideal but it can be supported and led up to by careful use of extrinsic rewards and praise.
- The lower-level needs of students, such as hunger, thirst or security, need to be met before higher-level needs can become the student's primary goal.

- Boosting self-esteem and developing feelings of 'self-efficacy' rather than 'learned helplessness' is a vitally important goal.
- Expectations and aspirations (by students and teachers) are key factors relating to motivation and therefore to achievement.

Finally, one of the important activities to have emerged in relation to motivation is the business of *goal setting* or *target setting*. Target setting for pupils is a means of boosting their confidence, encouraging them to take responsibility for their own learning and eventually to raise their achievement. It can often be done as a result of **formative assessment**. The idea underlying target setting is that students should negotiate goals with the teacher which are: clear and specific, moderately difficult, and achievable in the near future. By achieving those goals, and being given feedback on and praise for them, self-esteem and motivation are raised. One useful acronym for remembering the key features is SMART. Goals which are 'SMART' will be *S*pecific, *M*easurable, *A*ttainable, *R*ealistic and *T*imebound.

References and further reading

Bandura, A. (1992) 'Perceived Self-Efficacy in Cognitive Development and Functioning', *Educational Psychologist*, 28: 117–48.

Berk, L. (2003) *Child Development*, Boston: Allyn and Bacon.

Dwek, C. (2000) *Self-Theories: Their Role in Motivation, Personality and Development*, Philadelphia, PA: Psychology Press.

Maslow, A. ([1943] 1987) *Motivation and Personality*, 3rd edn, New York: Harper and Row.

Weiner, B. (1980) 'The Role of Affect in Rational (Attributional) Approaches to Human Motivation', *Educational Researcher*, 9: 4–11.

——(1992) *Human Motivation: Metaphors, Theories and Research*, Newbury Park, CA: Sage.

Useful websites

http://www.garysturt.free-online.co.uk/motivat2.htm
   On learned helplessness:
http://ematusov.soe.udel.edu/final.paper.pub/_pwfsfp/00000062.htm
http://www.dmu.ac.uk/~jamesa/learning/learned_helplessness.htm
   On intrinsic motivation:
http://education.calumet.purdue.edu/vockell/EdPsyBook/Edpsy5/Edpsy5_intrinsic.htm
http://www.nmsa.org/research/res_articles_sept2001.htm
   On attribution theory:

http://mentalhelp.net/psyhelp/chap4/chap4k.htm
http://www.as.wvu.edu/~sbb/comm221/chapters/attrib.htm
   Maslow's original (1943) classic paper can be seen at:
http://psychclassics.yorku.ca/Maslow/motivation.htm
   Several sites on motivation can be found via the National Key Stage 3
Strategy website of the DfES:
http://www.standards.dfes.gov.uk/keystage3/search/?mode = basic_search&
   pagenumber = 1&d = m-ks3&search_string = motivation

MULTIPLE INTELLIGENCES

Views of 'intelligence' as a concept changed dramatically through
the last century (see **intelligence**). The early twentieth-century
model of 'IQ' (intelligence quotient) as a measurable, constant
entity that characterised a child's or adult's ability to think became
discredited for all sorts of good reasons, not least because the
'intelligence test' that allegedly claimed to measure intelligence was
often shown to be culturally and racially biased. It can now be
said that the only thing that intelligence tests of the twentieth
century succeed in measuring is our aptitude in carrying out
intelligence tests.

   The concept of multiple intelligences posits that human 'ability' is
made up of a wide range of different 'intelligences', which may be
present in differing degrees. Each intelligence is said to have its own
set of mental operations. There is no single, overarching mental
ability (once called 'g'). The idea or theory of multiple intelligences is
often associated with the American psychologist Howard Gardner.
He postulated the following list of 'intelligences':

- *interpersonal*: the intelligence of social understanding – being able
  to appreciate and respond to the feelings, motivations and intentions of other people;
- *intrapersonal*: of self-knowledge, i.e. knowing and guiding one's
  own behaviour and feelings; recognising one's own strengths,
  weaknesses, intelligences and desires;
- *naturalist*: the ability to identify and classify things in the natural
  world, i.e. animals, plants and minerals;
- *verbal/linguistic*: of words, speech and language;
- *musical/rhythmic*: of tone, rhythm, pitch and timbre;
- *visual/spatial*: of pictures and images;
- *bodily/kinaesthetic*: of the whole body and hands;

- *logical/mathematical*: the intelligence of numbers and reasoning, detection of logical and numerical patterns; skill with long chains of logical or mathematical reasoning.

Gardner also proposed, in his later work, other intelligences such as spiritual and moral but these were less well defined and are more controversial.

One practical, positive aspect of this model of the human mind is that it can be used by teachers and parents to recognise and highlight or celebrate learners' particular strengths and abilities, perhaps raising confidence and self-esteem. A negative feature is that children could be categorised as having certain intelligences – this could lead (perhaps) to labelling and even stereotyping along gender or racial lines, e.g. boys as visual or spatial learners, girls as verbalisers. The theory, whether right or wrong, has also been used to boost children's self-esteem by identifying 'eight kinds of smart'. Children can then be told that they are one, some or perhaps all of the following:

- word smart (linguistic intelligence);
- number/reasoning smart (logical–mathematical);
- picture smart (spatial);
- body smart (bodily-kinaesthetic);
- music smart (musical intelligence);
- people smart (interpersonal);
- self smart (intrapersonal);
- nature smart (natural).

The multiple intelligences (MI) and 'smart' model is closely related to the current fashion to attribute learning styles or cognitive styles to different students. For example, one fad has been to distinguish three types of learner: *visual* (*V*), *auditory* (*A*) and *kinaesthetic* (*K*) (see **learning styles**). This VAK classification may well have been useful in encouraging teachers to recognise that different students learn in different ways (and differently on different days as every teacher and parent knows by intuition). For example, it can be used to check that different aspects of a lesson (V, A or K) are present in a given lesson and therefore highlighted on lesson plans. Where it becomes dangerous is when certain children are branded as one type of learner and this becomes a label (especially when they themselves use it – I have had children in Year 7, and post-graduates, say to me: 'I'm a kinaesthetic learner').

Advocates of the idea of multiple intelligences claim support for it from neurological and 'brain' science, e.g. with subjects where damage to one region of the brain has affected one ability, e.g. linguistic ability, but left others untouched. The existence of child and adult 'prodigies' (i.e. a person endowed with a certain amazing ability in one specific area such as mathematics or music), or even the 'idiot savant', is also alleged to support the theory.

But the concept of multiple intelligences has had its critics. White (1998), for example, argues that Gardner's theory is too narrow and intelligence is largely a result of experience. Another criticism is that the 'theory', appealing as it may be, has very little empirical evidence to support it. In addition, **emotional intelligence** and the affective domain (see **Bloom's taxonomy**) are now recognised as other vital facets in a learner's profile in determining her or his success in attainment.

Nevertheless, the idea of multiple intelligences could fairly be said to have encouraged teachers to think more broadly about learners' needs and that is surely a positive outcome, whatever the status of MI as a concept or 'theory'.

References and further reading

Gardner, H. (1993) *Intelligence Reframed: Multiple Intelligences for the 21st Century*, New York: Basic Books.

White, J. (1998) *Do Howard Gardner's Multiple Intelligences Add Up?* London: Institute of Education, University of London.

Useful websites

http://tip.psychology.org/gardner.html
http://www.education-world.com/a_curr/curr054.shtml
http://www.funderstanding.com/multiple_intelligence.cfm
http://www.infed.org/thinkers/gardner.htm
http://www.newhorizons.org/strategies/mi/front_mi.htm
http://www.thomasarmstrong.com/multiple_intelligences.htm

PASTORAL CARE AND PSHE

Pastoral care is usually associated with the welfare and well-being of students rather than their cognitive development (although a search of the World Wide Web clearly shows that the word 'pastoral' is most commonly related to the clergy, the pastor or priest).

In the 1960s it became common for secondary schools to divide teachers and their responsibilities into 'academic' and 'pastoral' (with the occasional gap in parity of esteem between the two). Two hier-archies and two career ladders began to develop. The school's frame-work for managing pastoral care became known as the pastoral system (Gordon and Lawton, 2003, p. 184), with its class tutors, tutor groups, heads of year (or sometimes house groupings) and heads of pastoral care. Similarly, in the academic world, separate journals developed on pastoral care in education (see the website below).

Now, in National Curriculum terms, pastoral care is often linked to the importance of pupils' spiritual, moral and social development. In schools, it tends to be connected with certain staff (the pastoral staff) and certain timetabled slots, e.g. PSE or PSHE (personal and social education/personal, social and health education). These ran, and still run, alongside the traditional National Curriculum subjects such as English, Science and Mathematics. More recently, **citizen-ship** education has been linked to pastoral care although it is actually a statutory subject in its own right in England and Wales.

PSHE

Many schools show evidence of exemplary coverage of pastoral care in the curriculum and provision for PSHE. But in others, PSHE has become something of a Cinderella subject (to use the cliché) due to its perceived low status, its position 'outside of the mainstream cur-riculum', and the fact that it is rarely assessed. In schools, PSHE les-sons are often taken by a tutor who is not a specialist (PSHE specialists seem to be a rarity) and who may be neither confident, equipped nor willing to deal with sensitive and controversial issues such as sex and drugs. PSHE is often 'squeezed' into the timetable and 'tutorial time' is often eroded by other school matters or student activities. Another issue for PSHE has been the advent of citizenship – how does PSHE sit alongside this relatively new, compulsory element of the curriculum? The intention was that the statutory citizenship subject should complement the non-statutory PSHE, but has this happened?

An Ofsted report in 2005 (25 January) stated that PSHE is still poor in many secondary schools and non-existent in others. Previous reports had found it 'patchy', with huge differences between schools. Yet the aims behind PSHE are of vital importance, especially to sec-ondary-aged children: the building of self-esteem, personal and emotional development, health education, preparation for parent-hood and confidence in tackling issues in future life – these are all essential aims of education. Equally, the school's role and responsibility in the social, moral and emotional development of children have been forced to expand in twenty-first-century society and are likely to grow still further as provision in schools is extended to cover more hours of the day (currently christened the 'Kelly Hours').

In some ways, it is unfortunate that the two domains of learning have been separated and divided as at present. The ideal situation would be for personal and pastoral care to be a part of every teacher's remit and to be incorporated into all curriculum subjects: the students' attitude, well-being and frame of mind are vitally important factors in their cognitive development. Equally, cognitive development and achievement can lead to a sense of well-being, better self-image and higher self-esteem. In practice, though, the diffusion of personal and pastoral education into all subjects has not occurred and the coming of Citizenship as a separate subject may reinforce this. As a result, the pastoral/academic division can clearly be seen in school timetables and within classrooms – and, indeed, in the teaching profession with jobs and positions of responsibility in pastoral care and career paths being mapped out along the 'pastoral route'.

It would be extremely unfortunate if our curriculum and professional structures ever lead to the position that a student's cognitive learning becomes separated from his or her pastoral care and personal development; or even more crudely that some teachers simply teach their subject, while others tend to the pastoral side of the student's education.

References and further reading

Calvert, M. and Henderson, J. (1998) *Managing Pastoral Care*, London: Cassell.
Gordon, P. and Lawton, D. (2003) *Dictionary of British Education*, London: Woburn Press.
Ofsted (2005) *Personal, Social and Health Education in Secondary Schools*, London: Ofsted.

Useful websites

http://www.curriculumonline.gov.uk/Subjects/PSHE/Subject.htm?cookie%5Ftest = 1
http://www.ofsted.gov.uk/publications/index. cfm?fuseaction = pubs.display file&id = 3828&type = pdf -
http://www.qca.org.uk/7835.html
http://www.teachernet.gov.uk/management/atoz/p/pshe/
    For journals dealing with pastoral care, see:
http://www.blackwellpublishing.com/journal.asp?ref = 0264–3944

PEER TUTORING

Basically, peer tutoring occurs when one student helps another with her or his work and learning, usually with guidance from the teacher. Peers are usually in the same age group but the term is sometimes used when tutor and tutee are of different ages ('cross-age tutoring'). Although peer tutoring has recently become more topical because it is seen as one means of raising achievement as part of the 'school improvement' and school effectiveness movement, it has been used as an educational aid for several centuries (see website below).

There is a range of definitions and examples of peer tutoring. It may occur when one peer is an expert and the other is a novice. But not all peer tutors are experts – in many class situations it occurs with randomly assigned classmates in the same year group. In other definitions, cross-age tutoring may be ruled out because, almost by definition, peers should be of a similar age. Peer and cross-age tutoring also go by the names of 'peer teaching', 'peer education', 'partner learning', 'peer learning', 'child-teach-child', and 'learning through teaching'. Sometimes co-operative learning in small groups has been referred to as peer tutoring.

What are the benefits to pupils of carefully designed and teacher-guided peer tutoring? Most of the research on this started back in the 1980s and the 1990s, particularly in areas such as reading and mathematics. Studies and experience seem to indicate several benefits:

- improved social behaviour, peer relations and co-operation;
- the development of social skills (in all peers) and teaching skills (by the tutor);
- an improved classroom atmosphere and environment, e.g. an atmosphere of sharing, support and co-operation;
- improved learning, in both the cognitive domain (knowledge and understanding) and the affective (attitude, enjoyment, enthusiasm);
- improved self-esteem, in the tutor and perhaps the tutee.

Why does peer tutoring appear to work in classrooms? Several explanations have been offered, both anecdotally and from research studies. Peers are said to 'speak the same language', which helps with communication, empathy and therefore learning. The tutor can learn alongside the tutor, according to the old adage: you don't really learn a subject until you have to teach it. Finally, students may often listen to their peers and be influenced by them, in a way that may not occur with a teacher or other adult – peer relationships and 'peer pressure' can have a strong influence on achievement. If used and harnessed in the *right* way, peers can make a positive difference in a school.

Thus, peer tutoring has a long history and would seem to have tremendous potential to improve learning, develop positive attitudes and raise achievement. It is also said to be highly cost-effective when compared with other innovations or interventions. Why then is it not more widely used in schools, especially when it appears to be a common feature of learning in industry and commerce? One explanation involves suspicion. Teachers may be, quite rightly, sceptical about its value. Equally, parents and school governors may mistrust and even raise objections to its use. The traditional job of the teacher is to be in authority and to transmit knowledge in a linear path from expert to novice. That is what they are seen as being paid for, this is the unwritten but powerful contract. Until this model of teaching shifts, then school pedagogy will commonly remain as it has done for decades and will remain out of step with learning and teaching in other contexts such as industry and commerce as well as being incongruent with the 'knowledge economy' and 'learning society' that politicians are trying to promote.

Further reading

Benard, B. (1990) *The Case for Peers*, Portland, OR: Northwest Regional Educational Laboratory.

Useful websites

http://www.addchoices.com/peer_tutoring.htm
http://ali.apple.com/ali_sites/ali/exhibits/1000328/Peer_Tutoring.html
http://www.ncrel.org/sdrs/areas/issues/students/atrisk/at6refer.htm
http://www.nwrac.org/pub/library/c/c_case.pdf
    On the history of peer tutoring, see:
http://www.nwrel.org/scpd/sirs/9/c018.html
    A 'digest' of research on peer and cross-age tutoring can be found at:
http://www.indiana.edu/~reading/ieo/digests/d78.html

POST-MODERNISM

This is a term that has become fashionable in some quarters but which is almost (by definition, as you will see below) impossible to define. The term begs the questions: what is 'modernism' and when did the modern era end and the post-modern begin? Again, this is impossible to specify. One account (from a scientist's point of view) is that post-modernism began in 1922 with the publication of the German scientist Werner Heisenberg's 'Uncertainty Principle'. This (in brief) stated that it is impossible to know both the exact position and the movement of a particle, because the means of observing it will affect that which is being observed. This ended the scientists' dream of a clockwork-style, mechanistic universe which could be predicted and measured – the myth of perfect predictability and certain truth ended there and then. Interestingly, the concept of the observer affecting the observed is now prevalent (quite rightly) in the social sciences in the so-called 'post-positivist' era that we now inhabit ('positivism' being the belief that 'true knowledge' can be obtained from observable phenomena only).

Others have suggested that post-modernism arrived with the advent of 'Chaos theory'. Chaos theory became well known through the saying: 'A butterfly flapping its wings in Australia may lead to a storm in Europe' (Gleick, 1993). A slight exaggeration perhaps but attention grabbing – to put chaos theory simply, small changes in one part of a system can have unforeseeable, unpredictable yet massive effects in another part. In essence, the universe is not predictable.

The two eras (if they can be called that) have been characterised as follows (Table 4). The characteristics of post-modernism can be described as:

- fragmentation;
- diversity;
- denial of empiricism (except in a localised context) and positivism;
- rejection of possible unifying theories in favour of 'multiple' theories;
- rejection of absolutes: no single rational, moral or theoretical framework;
- celebration of differences (without necessarily implying tolerance);
- recognition that all discourses are saturated with power or dominance;
- acceptance that there can be no neutral arbiters of 'truth' or knowledge (i.e. knowledge is not only theory-laden; it is also value-laden).

With the shift towards post-modernism came the following changes in our view of the world and our theories about how we know about it (i.e. our epistemology):

159

Table 4 Characteristics of modernity and post-modernity

Modernity	Post-modernity
mechanistic	probabilistic
deterministic	doubt
progress	uncertainty
rationality	pluralism
certainty	complexity

- Universal certainty and truth are replaced by multiple conceptions, local versions of 'truth' or 'multiple realities'.
- No one way of knowing is given higher authority or greater privilege over another (Agger, 1990).
- A clear boundary or distinction between subject and object becomes a blurring of 'knower' and 'known'; there is no clear division between subjectivity and objectivity.
- Scientific certainty becomes 'situated certainty':

Scientific certainty, the certainty grounded in proven principles of generalised applicability, is being replaced by situated certainty: the certainty that teachers and others can collectively glean from their shared practical knowledge of their immediate context and the problems it presents.

(Hargreaves, 1994, p. 59)

The idea of post-modernism has its critics and has attracted plenty of scepticism; whatever view one holds on the notion, it certainly will be part of the debate about education, knowledge and learning and their purposes in the twenty-first century.

References and further reading

Agger, B. (1990) *The Decline of Discourse: Reading, Writing and Resistance in Post-modern Capitalism*, Lewes: Falmer.

Appignanesi, R. and Garratt, C. (1995) *Post Modernism for Beginners*, Cambridge: Icon Books.

Gleick, J. (1993) *Chaos: Making of a New Science*, London: Abacus.

Hargreaves, A. (1994) *Changing Teachers, Changing Times*, London: Cassell, especially pp. 48–85.

Lyotard, J-F. (1984) *The Post-Modern Condition: A Report on Knowledge*, Minneapolis: University of Minnesota Press.

Usher, R. and Edwards, R. (1994) *Post Modernism and Education*, London: Routledge.

Useful websites

http://www.as.ua.edu/ant/Faculty/murphy/436/pomo.htm
http://www.infed.org/biblio/b-postmd.htm
http://en.wikipedia.org/wiki/Postmodernism

PROBLEM-BASED LEARNING

Problem-based learning (PBL) is a teaching strategy in which a problem is used to 'drive' the learning. It is said that presenting students with a real-life problem to suggest a solution can be highly motivational; some go further in suggesting that PBL can provide a new, motivating opportunity for pupils who have not done well in traditional, didactic teaching situations.

The origins of PBL (and inquiry-based learning) go back to at least the 1960s when medical students were set problems to solve as part of their medical training. It has since been used widely in higher education and more recently in secondary schools.

Students are presented with real-world, unstructured, perhaps 'messy' problems that may have a range of viable solutions. Their aim is to research, devise, evaluate and present one possible solution or at least a strategy for addressing the problem (they are unlikely to come up with a 'solution', if the problem is 'real').

This will involve certain well-guided stages, for example:

Stage 1: *Meeting and setting out the problem*: students are presented with a real-world situation or problem. They begin, with guidance from the teacher, by asking: What do I know already about this problem or question? What do I need to know to address this problem and come up with a suggested strategy or perhaps a solution? What resources can I access to do this?

Stage 2: *Searching for, weighing up and making use of information*: once they have grasped and understood the problem, pupils then search for and access resources of as many kinds as possible: print-on-paper, other humans, the Internet and other electronic sources. They must then evaluate the resource or source: is it up to date? How trustworthy, credible and accurate is it? Is there any reason to suspect bias in the source?

Stage 3: *Suggesting a solution and presenting it*: at this stage, students construct a solution to the problem. Students may then be asked to report on their strategy and to present it to a group, perhaps using multi-media.

These stages are best seen as cyclical rather than linear, for example, after the presentation/reporting stage, they may return to stage 1 by reconsidering the problem and what they need to know or find out in order to address it further.

PBL requires a shift in teaching and learning approach. The teacher becomes a guide, facilitator, and a resource provider as well as a potential source of information on a subject. This replaces the traditional teacher role as 'fount of all knowledge' or 'deliverer'. PBL also places a new onus on the learner, who must change from being receptive to being active – more independence, responsibility and self-direction will be demanded. This is especially true if pupils work collaboratively in small groups – they have a responsibility to other group members as well as themselves and will perhaps be motivated by some peer pressure.

PBL requires students to access and acquire knowledge but PBL is also said to develop the higher-order skills of critical thinking, application, evaluation and synthesis of knowledge and understanding (see **Bloom's taxonomy**). It can also develop the ability to work co-operatively with others in a team and the skill of problem solving (both currently described as **key skills**). A key feature of PBL, often seen as an important advantage over traditional teaching, is the motivating effect on students of working on an activity that is meaningful to them (for this reason, problem selection is a crucial part of this learning approach).

At present, PBL is not widely used in secondary schools, but it has gained widespread acceptance in higher education in fields far removed from medicine, where it originated. Its use in the school context is likely to grow.

Further reading

Boud, D. and Felleti, G. (1991) *The Challenge of Problem-Based Learning*, London: Kogan Page.

Savin-Baden, M. (2003) *Facilitating Problem-Based Learning: Illuminating Perspectives*, Maidenhead: SRHE and Open University Press.

Stepien, W. J. and Gallagher, S. A. (1993) 'Problem-based Learning: As Authentic as It Gets', *Educational Leadership*, 50(7): 25–8.

Woods, D. R. (1994) *Problem-Based Learning: How to Gain the Most from PBL*, Hamilton, ON: Donald R. Woods, Publisher.

Useful websites

http://eduscapes.com/tap/topic43.htm
http://mentalhelp.net/psyhelp/chap4/chap4k.htm
http://score.rims.k12.ca.us/problearn.html

REFLECTIVE PRACTICE

The idea of reflective practice and the 'reflective practitioner' has been popular since the 1980s and 1990s, especially as a result of the work of Donald Schön (Schön, 1983), becoming almost a buzzword in some circles. The concept has been applied to a range of professions, from nursing and physiotherapy to law and architecture. It has now become almost part of the definition of what it means to be a 'professional' and also the main process by which professionals learn and grow. For teachers, reflective practice starts with critical reflection on and examination of their own deeply held ideas and assumptions about their teaching – they question their own 'taken-for-granted assumptions'. In a real situation, such as a school, reflective practitioners continually evaluate the effects of their choices and actions on others (especially the pupils) and actively take advantage of opportunities to develop professionally.

The idea of reflective practice has had a huge influence on teacher education, both initial and in-service. Many courses internationally were redesigned in the late twentieth century in order to develop the 'reflective practitioner' (RP). The old model (if it ever existed) of 'provide them with the research and theory and then send them out to teach' is now seen as flawed. The RP model stresses the importance of learning by experience – learning by doing and reflecting on it. This is achieved by both 'reflection-in-action' (thinking on your feet) and 'reflection-on-action'. The latter occurs after the event – it involves looking back and reflecting on what occurred e.g. during a lesson, and engaging in what Schön calls 'reflection on reflection-in-action'. In some ways it is analogous to **metacognition** – in this context, it means thinking about teaching as much as thinking about learning.

RP does require self-examination and introspection; it requires the teachers to think about their own practice and learn from it. But it should also involve three other features:

- Coaching and mentoring by a more experienced professional, who is also a reflective practitioner. Professionals new to a field can learn by observing others, by being observed themselves and by entering into a dialogue about both sets of practice.
- Working with and learning with and from peers (sometimes called 'peer reflective groups'): once again, dialogue is essential.
- Reading and learning from literature and research, which can be used to help reflect on practice and improve it.

Reflective practice is now widely accepted in several professions as a basis for a healthy profession and a means of continuing professional development and growth (see **continuing professional development**). Its stress is on learning from experience and healing the old split between theory and practice, or research and practice. The reflective practitioner is a researcher in her or his own right. This should lead to three benefits: (1) a deeper understanding of teaching; (2) a 'healthier' profession; and (3) improved effectiveness.

References and further reading

Boud, D. and Walker, D. (1998) 'Promoting Reflection in Professional Courses: The Challenge of Context', *Studies in Higher Education*, 23(2): 191–206.

Brookfield, S. D. (1995) *Becoming a Critically Reflective Teacher*, San Francisco: Jossey-Bass.

Schön, D. A. (1983) *The Reflective Practitioner: How Professionals Think in Action*, New York: Basic Books.

——(1987) *Educating the Reflective Practitioner: Toward a New Design for Teaching and Learning in the Professions*, San Francisco: Jossey-Bass.

Useful websites

Atherton, J. S. (2003) *Learning and Teaching: Reflective Practice [On-line]* UK: http://www.dmu.ac.uk/~jamesa/learning/reflecti.htm
http://www.ericdigests.org/2001-3/reflective.htm
http://educ.queensu.ca/~russellt/howteach/reflect.htm

SECONDARY EDUCATION

Secondary education is the stage between the primary or elementary phase of education and higher or university education. Secondary schooling has a long history and there is now a wide range of different types of secondary school, other than the category that one government spokesman in the late twentieth century called the 'bog standard comprehensive school' (see website below).

The past 100 years have seen the 'tripartite system' (see later), the City Technology College (CTC), the Academy and the specialist comprehensive school (see website below). This is in the state sector alone. In the fee-paying sector we have private schools, which still persist, and the oddly named 'public schools' which are also fee-paying but which enjoy a privileged 'charitable' status going back for centuries and are largely exclusive and private. Critics of the current multiplicity (myself included) argue that secondary schools cannot really be called 'comprehensive' while this range, with its selection either according to ability to pay or the alleged 'ability' of its students, exists alongside them. The rhetoric behind this range of provision usually depends on arguments about freedom of opportunity and parental choice – fine if you have the money to pay for them and you live in an area that can offer this 'freedom'.

The fact that the secondary stage of schooling is sandwiched between the primary phase and further/higher education raises one of the major tensions in secondary schooling; for some pupils, it is their final stage of education (before work or work training) but for others it is a preparation for extended education. What implications does this have for the curriculum, the teaching and learning, and the assessment system of secondary education?

There are several recurrent questions for secondary schooling that have never been resolved:

1 Who is secondary education for and what is its purpose? Has it yet evolved from being an education for 'an elite' to a comprehensive education for every pupil? Secondary schooling cannot escape from its long history and set of traditions going back to the ideas of a 'liberal, general education' for the elite, i.e. the professional middle classes. The origins of these ideals are said to lie in the liberal education of the Greeks, notably Plato and Aristotle. Liberal education is said to be about *improvement* rather than *use* (Pring, 1995, pp. 184–6) with its chief aim being to develop the intellect, to improve the capacity to think and understand and to appreciate what is worthy of appreciation. But do these liberal ideals still hold now that, over the past century, the secondary school has evolved into an institution for everybody? So there are ongoing debates and tensions about what it is for and for whom: how can its 'elite functions' and the old but persistent idea of a general, liberal education sit alongside the newer broader, more comprehensive purposes of secondary education for all?

2 Should the curriculum be the same for all or designed to provide something for everyone? The curriculum of the Middle Ages was based on the seven liberal arts: the 'trivium' of grammar, rhetoric and dialectic, and the 'quadrivium' of geometry, arithmetic, astronomy and music. In some ways the twenty-first-century **curriculum** reflects these traditions, with its distinctly separated subject boundaries and separate 'disciplines'. Is this appropriate for

a century in which most research and work-based activity is multi-disciplinary? Does it make sense to offer the same 'diet' to all pupils, whatever their interests or abilities? Some have argued for a 'segmented curriculum', a version of horses for courses, e. g. one pathway for the 'academic pupil' and one for the non-academic; or going back to the late nineteenth century, but still persisting, separate curricula to meet the supposedly different requirements of boys and girls in later life. But will 'segmentation' simply create more divisions?

3 Should there be separate schools according to interest, aptitude and 'ability'? Different types of secondary schools for different types of ability or orientation were developed in the so-called 'tripartite' system of grammar, technical and modern schools put forward in 1944 in England but these are said to have fostered inequality and stifled opportunity in a striking way (McCulloch, 1998). Recently in the UK, we have seen a growing movement towards specialisation of secondary schools leading to so-called **specialist schools**, focusing on and receiving funding for one area, e.g. science, the arts, technology. How can these be reconciled with the ideal of a general, comprehensive, balanced and liberal education for all pupils?

4 Is the purpose of secondary schooling to provide a 'liberal education' or to prepare people for employment? How can the original 'liberal ideals' of secondary education sit side by side with its vocational function, i.e. if it forms a preparation for higher education for some students but a preparation for work for others? Will there ever be 'parity of esteem' between vocational education and academic education, especially if they lead to two distinct sets of qualifications at the end of secondary schooling?

The comprehensive ideal for secondary schooling is now widespread but inequalities of opportunity, achievement and entry to higher education have remained largely unchanged. Despite so-called 'widening participation' in HE, the percentage of students entering HE from the middle classes has stayed constant. In effect, participation has greatly expanded (in number terms) but can hardly be said to have widened. Expanded participation should not be mistaken for widening participation. This can be seen in the massive gap between the top constituency in England and Wales for university participation rates in 2005, Kensington and Chelsea with 69 per cent, and the lowest at only 8 per cent (an area in Nottingham). Within one city alone, there existed a gap of 54 per cent between the Sheffield

Hallam constituency (at 62 per cent participation in HE) compared with an area less than 6 miles away, Sheffield Brightside, at only 8 per cent (all figures from HEFCE).

The continuing debates about the purposes of secondary schooling can be seen as a kind of eternal triangle, with tensions between its three key features at each apex: curriculum, pedagogy and assessment (see Figure 7).

The ongoing debates about the range and type of subjects that should be included in the secondary school curriculum, the ways in which they should be taught (pedagogy) and how they should be assessed are all inter-related. Assessment affects teaching (often said to be the tail wagging the dog); equally, a nationally laid down curriculum affects both pedagogy (often making it a process of 'delivery') and assessment. The influences, the pushes and pulls between the three are mutual. The key question for secondary schools is how to cater for all types of pupil in their examinations/assessment, pedagogy and curriculum. This question has a long history but the tensions over the purposes and the curriculum of secondary education are certain to remain. How should it be taught and to whom? How should the curriculum be tested and examined? The key questions for the higher education and employment that lie beyond secondary education are equally hard to resolve: in what ways are the pedagogy, curriculum and assessment procedures of secondary education either preparing students for employment in the so-called 'knowledge society' or for becoming lifelong learners? At present the teaching styles, curriculum and assessment systems of the secondary school can

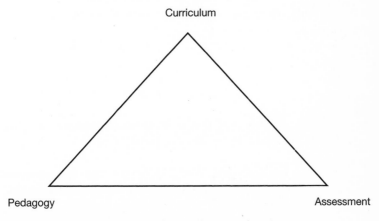

Figure 7 Tensions between curriculum, pedagogy and assessment

hardly be said to be an ideal preparation for life and work in the society that is now developing.

References and further reading

McCulloch, G. (1998) *Failing the Ordinary Child? The Theory and Practice of Working Class Secondary Education*, Buckingham: Open University Press.

Pring, R. (1995) *Closing the Gap: Liberal Education and Vocational Preparation*, London: Hodder and Stoughton.

Useful websites

http://www.anglaisfacile.com/free/civi/Educationr.htm
    On 'Academies':
http://www.standards.dfes.gov.uk/academies/
    On specialist schools:
http://www.standards.dfes.gov.uk/specialistschools/
    On the 'bog standard' quote, see:
http://www.worldwidewords.org/qa/qa-bog1.htm

SITUATED COGNITION AND SITUATED LEARNING

The premise underlying 'situated cognition' is that learning takes place, and knowledge and understanding are acquired, in different contexts and situations. The strong thesis is that all cognition (i.e. skills, ability and understanding) is dependent on the context that it was acquired in; and it does not readily transfer to other contexts or other situations. The debate over whether cognition is situated or not is linked to the debate over transfer of learning and the idea of learning communities. The key question for those who believe in situated cognition is: can skills, knowledge and understanding learnt in one context transfer to another, very different context? Or is cognition situated-dependent and context-dependent?

Those who argue the case that all learning and cognition are situated base their view on the following claims:

● Learning is fundamentally social and cultural (not individual and impersonal). It is the situation that counts, not the subject matter. The focus then shifts from what is learned to *how* it is learned, *where and with* or *through whom*.

- The community of learners is vitally important, e.g. as in the apprenticeship model of learning. Learners become part of a **community of practice** (see the work of Lave and Wenger, 1991a, 1991b); initially they are on the periphery of this community – as they learn and become socialised into it they move from this 'legitimate peripheral participation' (Lave and Wenger's term) to more central involvement.
- As a result, the following roles become vitally important: coaching, mentoring, showing, getting 'a feel for things', trying things out and practising. The focus is on participation, not reception and transmission.
- The focus in learning should be on social and community aspects, not the individual's mind/brain (i.e. the shift is from the individual as a unit of analysis to the socio-cultural setting, the community).

Protagonists such as Lave (1988) argue that there is little evidence of people's ability to apply knowledge they gain in one context to problems they encounter in another. This implies that the so-called core or key skills, e.g. problem solving, are not transferable.

Those who argue against the idea of situated learning argue for the claim that cognition (i.e. skills, knowledge and understanding) can transfer from one context to another. They argue that to teach and learn in the 'right way' can improve the chances of transfer occurring. This would involve:

- teaching and learning for understanding – as opposed to rote-learning, following specific rules without knowing why, etc.;
- using lots of examples and situations in teaching and learning, i.e. multiple contexts;
- helping students to reflect on their own learning and how they achieved it, i.e. metacognition; preparation for future learning should be seen as the aim of all teaching and learning.

The debate has been going for a long time – the jury is still out.

Types of knowledge and ways of learning

Linked to the above 'split', although slightly different, is the alleged dichotomy between academic learning and 'work-based learning', and similarly between academic knowledge and vocational knowledge. Some of the possible characteristics of these dichotomies are shown, in very polarised form, in Tables 5 and 6.

Table 5 Ways of learning

Academic learning	Work-based learning
Largely solitary study	Working with others
Uninterrupted work	Constant distractions
Concentration on single discipline or subject: depth	Different levels across different disciplines: breadth, multi-disciplinary
Much written work	Many oral, interpersonal skills needed
High analytical ability	Problem-solving, decision-making
Requires self-discipline	Motivating and stimulating

Table 6 Types of knowledge

Academic	Vocational
Theory	Practice
Knowledge'that'/why	Knowledge 'how'
Disembedded	Embedded
Universalisable	Situational
Independent of context	Context-dependent
Off-the-job	*In situ*/on-the-job
Abstract	Concrete
Conceptual	Procedural
'Academic' knowledge	Knowledge-in-action
Verbalised	Difficult to verbalise (tacit)
Higher currency	Lower currency and esteem

Some people will not agree with these characteristics – they are probably an over-exaggeration of the differences. But this polarisation does serve to highlight different aspects of learning and teaching and different 'types of knowledge' that go towards making up a truly balanced secondary curriculum.

Are there any 'general, educable' skills or other aspects of cognition?

Figure 8 is inspired by Adey's (1997) article on the search for skills that can have general value and transfer from one situation to another. It has two axes: one goes from Educable at the top to 'Not educable' at the bottom; the other axis runs from General at the right, to Specific (context dependent) at the left. The key question is: which of our attitudes, behaviours and cognition can be placed in this figure? In which quadrant should they be placed? For example, human reflexes and instincts have been placed in the bottom left quadrant – are they really specific and non-educable? Skills and knowledge that are said to be 'hard-wired' into our brains or innate could be placed in the bottom right quadrant. Is this correct? Should inherited intelligence (if there is such a thing) go in here? The quadrant that Adey's article is really concerned with is the top right – are there any general, educable skills (or other cognition) that could be placed here? This is what I would call the 'optimistic quadrant'! The top-left quadrant could be said to be the 'Training' section: is this where we should place specific skills that people can be taught to perform?

How useful is Figure 8 in showing human *attitudes*? Can attitudes be taught or are we 'stuck with them' from birth? How does this figure relate to the 'nature versus nurture' (genetics versus environment) debate? Does it shed any light on it? Which quadrant is most open to improvement by nurture and the environment?

Conclusion

This entry has raised questions about the idea that learning in formal education can transfer to, and therefore be a preparation for, future life or employment. 'Situated cognition' has become something of a cult now, with websites devoted to it and certain books and articles seemingly determined to show that all cognition is situated and dependent on context. My own view is that reality lies somewhere in the middle ground between the two poles, i.e. those at one end with

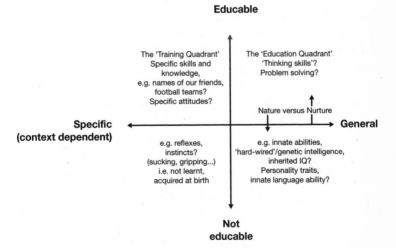

Figure 8 How 'generalisable' and 'educable' are cognition and attitudes?

an implicit belief in transfer and those at the other pole who wish to claim that all cognition is inevitably situated.

References and further reading

Adey, P. (1997) 'It All Depends on the Context, Doesn't It? Searching for General, Educable Dragons', *Studies in Science Education*, 29: 45–92.

Brown, S. J., Collins, A. and Duguid, P. (1989) 'Situated Cognition and the Culture of Learning', *Educational Researcher*, January–February: 32–42.

Lave, J. (1988) *Cognition in Practice*, Cambridge: Cambridge University Press. (Relates arithmetic problem-solving to daily life and shows how mathematical skill is used in the real world.)

Lave, J. and Wenger, E. (1991a) 'Legitimate Peripheral Participation in Communities of Practice', in Lave, J. and Wenger, E. *Situated Learning: Legitimate Peripheral Participation*, Cambridge: Cambridge University Press.

Lave, J. and Wenger, E. (1991b) *Situated Learning: Legitimate Peripheral Participation*, Cambridge: Cambridge University Press.

Rogoff, B. and Lave, J. (eds) (1984) *Everyday Cognition: Its Development in Social Context*, Cambridge, MA: Harvard University Press.

Useful websites

There are tens of thousands of websites available as you will see if you type 'situated cognition' into Google, for example. One useful summary of some of the available web-based resources can be found at: http://homepage.mac.com/scottlab/situated.html

SPECIALIST SCHOOLS

Different governments around the world have been experimenting with different types of secondary school since secondary education began. In England and Wales the 'Specialist Schools Programme' began in 1994 and by 2005 the majority of secondaries were Specialist Schools. Ten areas of specialism were open to schools to develop: technology, languages, science, engineering, sports, arts, business and enterprise, mathematics and computing, music and humanities. Schools can combine two specialisms.

The rhetoric behind the programme is that schools should be allowed to work to their strengths and the adoption of a specialism should lead to raising standards. The specialist department or faculty should take the lead in working across the school as part of a whole school improvement programme. Schools should also work with the local community, including feeder primary schools. One of the obvious benefits to schools is an improvement in their funding and therefore facilities and resources. Another benefit has been through the 'Specialist Schools Trust', the registered charity set up as the lead advisory body for the programme. This has created a large network of secondary schools (over 2,000 in 2005) which includes non-specialist schools. They work together in sharing good practice and in collaborative projects.

One of the DfES sites states:

> The Specialist Schools Programme helps schools, in partner-ship with private sector sponsors and supported by additional Government funding, to establish distinctive identities through their chosen specialisms and achieve their targets to raise standards.
>
> (http://www.standards.dfes.gov.uk/specialistschools/)

For schools which have become 'specialist', there are tangible improvements. However, certain questions can be raised about the programme:

- What if a school's strengths change over time? For example, with movement of staff, a new head teacher, the development of new areas of enthusiasm and excellence, or changes in the local community?
- In an era when the emphasis is on personalised learning and individual **learning styles**, can a specialist school's strengths match the pupils' strengths and learning preferences?
- How does an emphasis on one specialism sit alongside a compulsory, broad and balanced National Curriculum for all pupils?
- Parental choice: if the local comprehensive is a Specialist School (and the only one for miles around), how does this tally with the idea of parents having a choice of the appropriate type of school for their child? (of course, in reality, in many areas, there is no parental choice anyway).
- More generally, is the specialist schools movement compatible with the comprehensive ideal?

Some say that the Specialist Schools Programme is the answer to the 'bog standard comprehensive' tag of the late 1990s but its success in achieving a broad and balanced education, with equal opportunities for all pupils, and a rise in standards is, as yet, not fully proven.

Useful websites

http://news.bbc.co.uk/1/hi/education/3856411.stm
http://www.schoolsnetwork.org.uk/
http://www.specialistschools.org.uk/
For an Ofsted evaluation:
http://www.ofsted.gov.uk/news/index.cfm?fuseaction = news.details&id = 1665

SPIRAL CURRICULUM

This is the idea that a course or curriculum should not be all in one direction and in a straight line (linear) but instead should be cyclical or move forwards in a spiral. Certain topics or areas should be covered at one level and then returned to later in a course or curriculum and even revisited again and again.

The idea of a curriculum being spiral rather than linear is usually attributed to Jerome Bruner (note that Bruner was also one of the leading figures in the emergence of **constructivism**). He believed that some of the 'big ideas' in education could be introduced to children at an early age and then returned to later, perhaps in a gradually more complex and detailed form. His belief was that any subject can be 'taught effectively in some intellectually honest form to any child at any stage of development'. Put another way: 'Any idea or body of knowledge can be presented in a form simple enough so that any particular learner can understand it in a recognisable form' (Bruner, 1966, p. 4).

This belief links to another of Bruner's useful ideas: 'scaffolding'. This is the word (metaphor) used to describe structured and carefully sequenced teaching and learning – it should be tailored to suit the learner, according to his or her 'readiness' to progress (one of Piaget's terms) and disposition to learn. Thus, a carefully thought out spiral curriculum will take into account children's prior learning, their readiness to learn a certain concept or key idea, and then the teacher will scaffold the teaching and learning accordingly. Teaching will be adjusted at higher levels of the spiral as conceptual development and maturity grow and then the idea could be presented in a more complex way. So the curriculum is organised to allow students to continually build upon what they have already learned.

Bruner (1960) felt strongly that a spiral curriculum would help to structure teaching and learning in schools around the big ideas: the 'great issues, principles and values that a society deems worthy of the educational concern of its members'. There is something of the 1960s in this sentiment but Bruner's values, his ambitious approach to teaching and his concept of a spiral are still worthy of respect in this more cynical age.

References and further reading

Bruner, J. S. (1960) *The Process of Education*, Cambridge, MA: Harvard University Press.

——(1966) *Toward a Theory of Instruction*, Cambridge, MA: Belknap Press.

——(1971) *The Relevance of Education*, New York: W. W. Norton.

——(1983) *Child's Talk: Learning to Use Language*, New York: W. W. Norton.

——(1986) *Actual Minds, Possible Worlds*, Cambridge, MA: Harvard University Press.

——(1990) *Acts of Meaning*, Cambridge, MA: Harvard University Press.

——(1996) *The Culture of Education*, Cambridge, MA: Harvard University Press.

Useful websites

http://starfsfolk.khi.is/solrunb/jbruner.htm_3.htm
http://www.infed.org/thinkers/bruner.htm

THINKING SKILLS

There has been a movement lasting more than three decades to include teaching and learning in schools which promotes 'thinking skills'. The idea underlying the movement is that there is a wide range of generic, transferable skills which are certainly 'learnable' and probably teachable – they are not innate and unchanging (see **intelligence)**, but can grow and develop in the right environment and with the right teaching and learning interventions.

What are thinking skills?

No two lists, provided by advocates of a thinking skills approach, seem to be the same. In other words, there is no clear consensus on what skills should be considered to be the skills required for thinking. Many of them seem to be based on **Bloom's taxonomy** with its hierarchy running from factual recall at the bottom to analysis and synthesis at the top, for example, recalling, comparing, classifying, inferring, generalising, evaluating, experimenting and analysing.

Some lists have stressed the importance of information skills such as finding information, organising information and analysing information. Other lists, or taxonomies, have started with the information skills and gone on to include others in different categories such as: information processing, enquiry skills, reasoning, creativity and evaluation. A range of other lists can be found and they include the following, in no particular order: goal setting, problem solving, remembering, decision-making, 'brainstorming' new ideas, observing, sequencing, classifying, comparing, predicting, inferring and finding evidence.

In many discussions of thinking skills, the importance of **meta-cognition** is stressed, i.e. thinking about thinking. Others have, quite rightly in my view, included the importance of dispositions and attitudes towards learning and thinking. Some have called these 'habits of mind' and include such qualities as: having the right inclination, being flexible, listening to others, being alert, being persistent and making a commitment. These relate more closely to the affective domain of Bloom's taxonomy than the cognitive domain.

Programmes designed to develop thinking skills

Over the past few decades a number of programmes have been developed and tried as part of the thinking skills movement, for example:

1 *Feuerstein's Instrumental Enrichment*: Feuerstein's Instrumental Enrichment (IE) (Feuerstein *et al.*, 1980) was developed over 40 years ago for use with low-performing Israeli adolescents but it is still well known and widely referred to.

2 *Higher Order Thinking skills (HOTs)*: this is usually credited to Stanley Pogrow and emphasises the development of the higher-order skills such as evaluation and synthesis.

3 *Cognitive Research Trust (CoRT) by Edward de Bono*: de Bono has written numerous books on thinking (see de Bono, 1970). His approach, especially such tools as 'thinking hats', is used in some schools. De Bono's definition of thinking includes six aspects: breadth, organisation, interaction, creativity, information and feeling, and action.

4 *Cognitive Acceleration through Science Education (CASE)*: Cognitive Acceleration through Science Education encourages children to move from concrete examples to abstract generalisations, and promotes 'bridging' into other subject areas (see **cognitive acceleration**).

5 *Philosophy for Children*: Philosophy for Children is associated with Matthew Lipman (1991) in the USA and has been developed in the UK by Fisher (1998). Lipman believed that children were 'natural philosophers'.

6 *The Somerset Thinking Skills Course*: The Somerset Thinking Skills Course (Blagg *et al.*, 1993) is a general thinking skills course.

Why adopt the thinking skills approach?

Many justifications or rationales have been presented for adopting a thinking skills approach and even taking it further by developing 'thinking classrooms' and 'thinking schools' in some cases:

- A curriculum driven by thinking skills is a far better preparation for future citizenship and work than one based on the learning of factual subject content.
- We live in an 'information society' with exponential growth of information, in which no one person could know all there is to know about an area – the important skill is not to acquire information but to be able to find it, organise it, evaluate it and apply it.
- Specific subject knowledge soon becomes out of date in a rapidly changing technological society; learning facts and factual recall are no longer as important as 'learning how to learn' and being taught how to think.
- Similarly, thinking skills are a prerequisite for people to cope in a complex, globalised, quickly evolving world; they will be needed for lifelong learning, the learning society and for active citizenship in a democracy.

In the school context, further support has been offered by those who claim that a thinking skills approach can play a part in 'school improvement' by raising achievement and improving the quality of learning. Supporters of the approach argue that it can be embedded or infused into the subject curriculum, e.g. in Science, Mathematics, Technology, History, Geography. Teaching the skills of thinking can be done in and through subjects. Equally, thinking skills can be taught in their own right, i.e. explicitly, directly and deliberately.

Conclusion

The thinking skills movement has been based on the idea that there are certain general, transferable skills that can be developed in learners and improved as a result of teaching and learning. There is growing evidence that the approach has worked in developing thinking and even improving examination results, although certain critics argue that the evidence is not conclusive. It is now a well-established movement and, at present, it seems certain to continue.

References and further reading

Blagg, N. (1991) *Can We Teach Intelligence? A Comprehensive Evaluation of Feuerstein's Instrumental Enrichment*, Hillsdale, NJ: Lawrence Erlbaum Associates.

Blagg, N. and Ballinger, M. (1989) 'The Somerset Thinking Skills', in Coles, M. J. and Robinson, J. (eds) *Teaching Thinking*, Bristol: Bristol Press.

Blagg, N. R., Lewis, R. E. and Ballinger, M. P. (1993) *Thinking and Learning at Work: A Report on the Development and Evaluation of the Thinking Skills at Work Modules*, Sheffield: Department of Employment.

Dawes, L., Mercer, N. and Wegerif, R. (2000) *Thinking Together: A Programme of Activities for Developing Thinking Skills*, Birmingham: Questions Publishing.

De Bono, E. (1970) *Lateral Thinking*, London: Penguin.

——(1992) *Teach Your Child to Think*, London: Penguin.

Feuerstein, R., Rand, Y., Hoffman, M. and Miller, R. (1980) *Instrumental Enrichment: An Intervention Program for Cognitive Modifiability*, Baltimore, MD: University Park Press.

Fisher, R. (1998) *Teaching Thinking: Philosophical Thinking in the Classroom*, London: Continuum.

Goleman, D. (1995) *Emotional Intelligence: Why it Can Matter More than I.Q.*, New York: Bantam Books.

Lipman, M. (1991) *Thinking in Education*, Cambridge: Cambridge University Press.

McGuinness, C. (1999) *From Thinking Skills to Thinking Classrooms: A Review and Evaluation of Approaches for Developing Pupils' Thinking*, Nottingham: DfEE.

Sharron, H. and Coulter, M. (1994) *Changing Children's Minds: Feuerstein's Revolution in the Teaching of Intelligence*, Birmingham: Questions Publishing Company.

Shayer, M. and Adey, P. (2002) *Learning Intelligence*, Buckingham: Open University Press.

Useful websites

One striking piece of evidence for the spread of 'thinking skills' is the sheer number of websites devoted to it. The selection below includes those that I consider to be valuable, carefully reasoned and well written:

http://www.adprima.com/thinkskl.htm
http://www.aea267.k12.ia.us/cia/framework/thinking/
http://www.literacytrust.org.uk/Database/thinking.html
http://www.nwrel.org/scpd/sirs/6/cu11.html
http://www.standards.dfes.gov.uk/thinkingskills/
http://www.teachingthinking.net/Thinkskills.htm
   For research on thinking skills in the UK, see:
http://www.ncl.ac.uk/ecls/research/education/tsrc/
   Can thinking skills be taught?
http://www.scre.ac.uk/scot-research/thinking/

TRANSFER OF LEARNING

A central issue in the debate on the purpose of secondary education concerns the question of whether or not skills or abilities learnt at school or college will be of value, or will *transfer* to a future workplace, higher education or everyday life. An implicit belief in transfer forms a cornerstone of the justification of schooling as a preparation for the future and for employment. A belief in transfer also underlies the movement in the past century to provide students with 'transferable skills' and the more recent worldwide drive for core or **key skills**. What evidence is there, however, that transfer of learning between school and future work or study does take place? What are the conditions under which transfer occurs, if at all? Can skills be transferred from one context to another?

What is transfer?

Transfer can be defined as the ability to utilise one's learning in situations which differ to some extent from those in which learning occurs; or alternatively, transfer may refer to the influence of learning in one situation or context upon learning in another situation or context (Ausubel and Robinson, 1969). This is a useful working definition. In addition, we can separate *transferable* skills (which are skills learned in one context but readily used in others) and *transfer* skills (which are higher-order strategies that help a student to apply what has been learned to new situations, i.e. to enable transfer to take place). There are several types of transfer. Two of the most important are:

- *Learning-to-learning transfer*: learning in one domain may enhance learning in another, e.g. by learning Latin does it become easier to learn French, or vice versa?

- *Learning how to learn*: the act of learning in one situation improves the ability to learn in another.

One, more general, way of classifying transfer is to describe it as lateral, sequential or vertical (Ausubel and Robinson, 1969). Lateral transfer occurs with learning at the same level as the initial learning but in a different context, e.g. if skills or understanding taught at school are employed in a new context out of school. Thus, the possibility of lateral transfer is particularly relevant in considering the vocational curriculum. Sequential transfer occurs if the skills, ideas or concepts taught in one context then have a relationship to the skills, etc., in the next learning situation. This type of transfer is particularly relevant for teachers in planning a course of study. Finally, vertical transfer occurs when learning at one level facilitates learning at a higher level. Again, this appears to have most relevance in the context of teaching a hierarchical subject such as maths or physics.

When does transfer take place?

The following summary presents the main points in the debate over transfer which appears to have been running for most of the last century and probably longer (views on transfer are said to date back to the Ancient Greeks):

- Rote learning is by definition unlikely to lead to transfer, although training in memorisation techniques can improve transfer.
- Transfer has been said to occur only where there are identical elements or common components in the original learning and the new task (based on a classic study by Thorndike in 1924).
- Thorough mastery of the original learning task or material is necessary for transfer.
- Transfer is more likely to take place if widely varying examples of the concept, principle or strategy being transferred are used in the learning/teaching process and if the link is made consciously, i.e. a variety of instances is needed in the original learning.
- A conscious, meaningful approach to learning/teaching is required for transfer to take place, especially if the original learning contains over-learned, automatised sub-skills.
- 'Interference' (or negative transfer) in the application of original learning to new situations often arises.

- Transfer is likely to be greater the more intelligent a student is – with students of 'lower intelligence' longer and more detailed effort will be required to facilitate transfer.

While there is some agreement on the seven points summarised above, the evidence in the literature seems to be problematic on the following issues:

- *Assessing the extent of transfer*: there is no easy way of assessing with any degree of confidence the extent of transfer from one context to another.
- *Motivation*: if teachers and trainers attempt to 'teach for transfer' by using general examples and a range of contexts, this may reduce the motivation of the learner, i.e. the removal of training and education from a specific context in an effort to achieve generality may reduce the learner's motivation, e.g. in teaching supposedly transferable skills such as problem solving or planning. A delicate balance is needed between specificity and generality.
- *Transfer skills*: much work still needs to be done on the metacognitive skills and strategies that underlie the ability to transfer. Little is known about how individuals succeed or fail to use higher-order 'plans' to enable transfer.
- *Higher-order transferable skills*: there is still little conclusive evidence to show that the very general skills and strategies such as 'learning to learn' and problem solving really do transfer from one context or domain to another. Faith in problem-solving skills and approaches has now become accepted orthodoxy in curriculum statements and even in the mission statements of schools and colleges. Yet there is little evidence that there is a 'universal problem-solving ability'. Nor is there evidence that problem-solving transfers from one subject to another, let alone from school or college to the workplace. Are people who solve problems successfully in one domain, e.g. nuclear physics, successful in solving problems in another? Everyday experience and anecdote would certainly suggest not.
- *Change and transferable skills*: one of the driving forces behind the renewed emphasis in the 1980s and 1990s on generic and transferable skills was the alleged rate of change of jobs, skill requirements, and skill half-life in the workplace. This has been particularly strong in the case of technological change and the skills associated with new technology. Yet there is little concrete information on the skills required to handle new technology or whether they are transferable.

Critics of transfer

Lave (1988) provides a valuable critique of accepted wisdom on learning transfer and concludes that 'when we investigate learning transfer across situations, the results are consistently negative'. Even if skills do transfer within an educational context, it cannot be assumed they will transfer from the educational context to the world outside. Lave poses the question: 'Why have learning transfer theory and its functionalist underpinnings endured for so long?' Why have the 'widely distributed views which compose a taken-for-granted world of problem-solving and learning transfer' persisted? Why has the belief in transfer persisted? Lave suggests: 'An important part of the answer surely lies in its key role in the organisation of schooling as a form of education and in justifications of relations between schooling and the distribution of its alumni into occupations' (ibid., p. 71). In other words, implicit belief in transfer underpins the notion that the functions of education are to meet the needs of industry and to pre-pare young people for employment. As suggested above, this implicit belief is problematic.

References and further reading

Ausubel, D. and Robinson, F. (1969) *School Learning: An Introduction to Edu-cational Psychology*, New York: Holt, Rinehart and Winston.
Lave, J. (1988) *Cognition in Practice*, Cambridge: Cambridge University Press.
Thorndike, F. L. (1924) 'Mental Discipline in High School Studies', *Journal of Educational Psychology*, 15: 1–22, 83–98.

Useful websites

http://coe.sdsu.edu/eet/articles/transferLearn/start.htm
http://www.nwlink.com/~donclark/hrd/learning/transfer.html

WORK EXPERIENCE

Work experience is an aspect of the secondary curriculum that is worth considering critically, simply because so many students world-wide are now engaged in it – either for short periods of two or three weeks, or longer-term placements. Work experience also occurs in courses of further and higher education and in schemes for young people who may have left formal education but are seeking employ-ment. But what is it? What is it for? Why has it been introduced into the curricula of so many schools and colleges? How has it evolved over the years?

What is work experience?

Work experience is literally what it says. With the help of industry and commerce, it provides young people with experience of the world of work while they are still at school. It has been said to help young people to do the following:

- learn how to manage a different environment from school or college;
- learn to work alongside adults;
- relate their education and training to future career choices and aspirations; clarify their own ideas of employment and view different jobs more realistically;
- develop and practise new skills;
- make use of skills and knowledge learnt at school in 'real' situations;
- gain an insight into how industry and commerce work;
- give pupils some insights into the 'routines' and expectations in work, e.g. regular attendance, punctuality, dress, responsibilities to others;
- provide opportunities for pupils to make relationships with adults in a working environment;
- increase pupils' self-confidence by enabling them to experience new circumstances other than those in school (and perhaps to make a fresh start).

How and why has work experience evolved?

When compulsory education began at the end of the last century there was little need for work experience. Children often had first-hand knowledge and experience, albeit with limited horizons, of the world of work, often by working with parents in factories, fields or other workplaces. Families tended to live close to their place of work and the large physical (and nowadays mental) separation between home/school and work or between work and leisure hardly existed. Contrast this with the situation in the twenty-first century when 'leisure' is a phenomenon (indeed an industry), commuting is the norm, and the separation between 'work' and 'home' is almost total. It is hardly surprising that many young people with working parents have little or no idea what their parents do for a living. This huge shift has taken place in a century and is one of the stronger arguments in favour of work experience. The move towards work experience as part of the curriculum goes back only just over 40 years, although perhaps the first person to mention work experience was J-J. Rousseau in *Emile* in 1762. There he urged that work experience should become a part of general education for developing 'intelligence, skills of observation, persistence and skill'.

Some of the key events and reports that helped to push WE into the secondary curriculum in the 1960s, the 1970s and the 1980s were as follows:

- 1963: the Newsom Report (HMSO, 1963) which suggested that 'the school programme, in the last year especially, ought to be deliberately outgoing' (ibid., p. 72) and that 'work experience is ... practicable or even desirable for the large majority of boys and girls' (ibid., p. 76).
- 1973: the Education (Work Experience) Act was passed 'to enable education authorities to arrange for children under school-leaving age to have work experience, as part of their education' and solely referred to work experience in the last year of compulsory schooling.
- 1974: the Department of Education and Science Circular 7/74, circulated to all schools, further clarified the legality aspect of work experience and detailed the aims as being that pupils 'should be given an insight into the world of work, its disciplines and relationships'. It should include pupils of all abilities and should *not* be 'designed as vocational training' or provided only for the less able pupils. It also stated that consultation with parents, employers, and teachers as well as the pupils was necessary if the placements were to be successful and outlined guidelines related to safety, payments, insurance and the co-operation of other teachers.
- 1983: the TVEI (Technical and Vocational Education Initiative) for 14–18 year olds was introduced and later extended to bring in all LEAs in 1989. One of its stated aims was to give young people the opportunity to have planned work experience with a number of local employers.

What happens in work experience?

During WE, students might be engaged in a variety of tasks, from dogsbody, tea-maker or doughnut-fetcher, on the one hand, to positions of genuine responsibility and value on the other. Watts, writing in Miller *et al.* (1991), provided a useful classification of the categories of activity that students may be engaged in during WE. This is summarised in Table 7.

This is a useful classification of five 'forms of work experience' and I'm sure it will ring true for those teachers/lecturers who have been involved in it. But, as Watts points out, students are often faced with a mixture in the course of two or three weeks:

> These five forms of work experience are not necessarily mutually exclusive, and it is possible to combine elements of two or more of them. For example, some element of rotating around different departments might be used in the early stages of a placement, as part of the induction process, before settling down to doing an actual job or helping someone in an actual job. Nonetheless, it is useful to tease out the pros and cons of each form, and indeed such an analysis might be useful in negotiating what form or forms a placement should take.
>
> (Watts, 1991, p. 28)

Making the most of work experience

Most advocates of work experience argue that WE will only have full value if it is made part of a cycle which includes careful observation and opportunity for reflection – arguably this has influenced, and raised the status of, the briefing and debriefing which now form part of every school's/college's WE programme. This cycle is based on Kolb's widely used and cited experiential cycle (see Figure 1 in **action research**).

Most schools and teachers in secondary schools now accept that WE is an important part of the later secondary curriculum, provided it is conceptualised in this way and the employers play their part in

---

Table 7 Forms of work experience

1 Doing an actual job.
2 Providing an 'extra pair of hands'.
3 Helping someone in an actual job.
4 Rotating around different departments.
5 Carrying out specifically constructed tasks.

---

making it worthwhile. Many employers now accept that for them it can be a valuable process, not least in allowing opportunity for in-house development of their own staff in a supervisory or mentoring role.

References and further reading

Kolb, D. A. (1984) *Experiential Learning*, Englewood Cliffs, NJ: Prentice-Hall.
Miller, A., Watts, A. and Jamieson, I. (eds) (1991) *Re-thinking Work Experience*, London: Falmer Press.
The Newsom Report (1963) *Half Our Future*, London: HMSO.
Watts, A. (1991) 'The Concept of Work Experience', in Miller, A., Watts, A. and Jamieson, I. (eds) *Re-thinking Work Experience*, London: Falmer Press.
Watts, A. (ed.) (1983) *The Future of Work Experience – and Work*, London: Heinemann.
Wellington, J. (1993) *The Work Related Curriculum*, London: Kogan Page.

Useful websites

http://www.cre.gov.uk/gdpract/ed_cop_ew_work.html
A Scottish study revealing sex stereotyping in work experience:
http://www.scre.ac.uk/spotlight/spotlight90.html
Guidance for schools:
http://www.schoolsnetwork.org.uk/item.asp?page = 226&item = 1743
A more general website on 'work-related learning' from the QCA:
http://www.qca.org.uk/14–19/6th-form-schools/68_188.htm
A critical report on work experience in 2005:
http://news.bbc.co.uk/1/hi/education/4619231.stm
DES circulars from the past can be found at:
http://www.education.ie/servlet/blobservlet/des_circular_listing.htm

ZONE OF PROXIMAL DEVELOPMENT

The zone of proximal development, sometimes called the ZPD or the Zo-ped, is the 'area' between the level at which students know something or can do something *on their own*, and the level of performance or skill they *could reach* given the right support, teaching or structured learning. This is a crucially important idea for the classroom teacher because it provides a way of visualising the area that they should be aiming at or constructing in their teaching – it is the area or zone where teachers should be 'pitching' their lesson. If they succeed in targeting this zone, teachers and mentors often say that they are 'pitching their lesson at the right level'. Another way of putting it is to call it the zone where there is a 'manageable level of difficulty' for the student (Berk, 2003, p. 258). It can also help to think of it as a zone of *potential* development.

The ZPD is an idea created by the Russian psychologist Lev Vygotsky. The ZPD is the zone between what the child or student already knows and where he or she could be if given the right kind of support and intervention by a teacher. This intervention might be direct teaching or it could be 'scaffolding', in which the right learning and teaching environment can gradually bring the student up to a higher level (just as scaffolding can enable a solid and permanent building to be constructed). The skill in scaffolding, and in teaching generally, involves breaking things down into manageable learning steps.

A slightly broader concept than scaffolding was given the term 'guided participation' (Rogoff, 1990, 1991). She used this idea to stress the importance of teacher/adult/parent and the learner in co-operating together in the ZPD.

The ideas of a 'zone' and 'scaffolding' are useful metaphors for considering learning at all levels. Teachers should aim to target the ZPD in order for progression to take place. If they aim too high, i.e. way above the 'target zone', then no learning will take place (except perhaps rote learning, 'parrot fashion'). If teachers aim too low, then the learner will not progress:

> Learning which is oriented toward developmental levels that have already been reached is ineffective from the viewpoint of the child's overall development. It does not aim for a new stage of the developmental process but rather lags behind this process.
>
> (Vygotsky, 1978)

Pitching learning and teaching at the right level is crucial for motivation and the affective domain: if there is no challenge, the learner is bored and apathetic; too much challenge leaves the learner frustrated and disaffected.

Figure 9 shows an illustration of the ZPD. The shaded zone, Region 1, represents the learner's current development. Region 2 is the ZPD representing the learner's potential development in the near future. As learning proceeds, a portion of the ZPD becomes part of the learner's present knowledge or skill and so a smaller ZPD remains. The arrows in Figure 9 represent learning, leading towards new development.

Vygotsky (1978) defined the ZPD as 'the distance between the actual development level as determined by independent problem solving and the level of potential development as determined through problem solving under adult guidance or in collaboration with more capable peers'. In other words, a student can perform a task under adult guidance or with peer collaboration that could not be achieved alone. The zone of proximal development bridges the gap between what is known and what can be known. Vygotsky claimed that learning occurred in this zone.

His view is that the social environment and social interaction, not least talking, is vital in promoting learning. The role of the teacher is to create this environment for learning to take place. Thought, language and learning go together. For scaffolding to be successful, it must provide step-by-step progression (no huge jumps), the correct 'pacing', a structured environment and (not least) motivation and interest for the learner.

Vygotsky's model of learning can apply as valuably to on-line (or e-) learning as it can in face-to-face situations. Students can use on-line communication to create a learning community, to collaborate

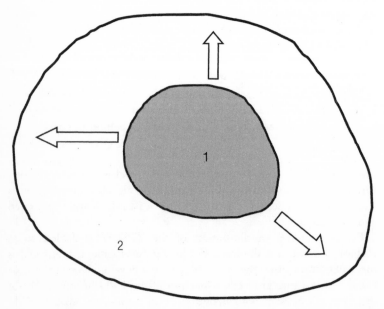

Figure 9 One way of picturing the ZPD

and to learn from each other – especially if this is facilitated by guidance and scaffolding by a teacher or on-line tutor.

Related ideas

The notion of a ZPD relates to, at the very least, two other ideas about learning. The first is **diagnostic assessment**: if teachers wish to pitch their lesson at the right level, i.e. in the ZPD, they need to know first the level that 'students are at'. The second is the idea of **meaningful learning**: learning will only be meaningful if it is pitched at the right level and built on a foundation of previous learning – scaffolding can help to make learning meaningful by taking learning up to the next storey in a sound and structured way, as opposed to jumping up to an unrealistic level which is unsupported, disconnected and left hanging in the air. As you can see, there is no limit to the metaphors that can be lifted from the construction industry in considering learning: foundations, bridging gaps, scaffolding, zones, storeys and things left hanging!!

One final important point about the ZPD is that it is not some sort of property or characteristic of the learner alone. It is certainly not some sort of entity or zone in the learner's brain that the teacher should 'aim at' – rather, it is an area or zone constructed by the interaction between the learner and the teacher or adult.

References and further reading

Berk, L. (2003) *Child Development*, 6th edn, Boston: Allyn and Bacon.

Rogoff, B. (1990) *Apprenticeship in Thinking*, New York: Oxford University Press.

——(1991) *Cognitive Development in Social Context*, Oxford: Oxford University Press.

Scaife, J. (2000) 'Learning in Science', in Wellington, J. (ed.) *Teaching and Learning Secondary Science*, London: Routledge.

Vygotsky, L. S. (1978) *Mind and Society: The Development of Higher Mental Processes*, Cambridge, MA: Harvard University Press.

Useful websites

There is a vast number of websites on the ZPD (try Google or Google Scholar to find several hundred). Two of the more readable and valuable are:

http://chd.gse.gmu.edu/immersion/knowledgebase/theorists/constructivism/vygotsky.htm

Too little challenge leaves the learner bored, and too much leaves him frustrated':
http://chss2.montclair.edu/sotillos/_meth/00000014.htm
For Barbara Rogoff's work, see:
http://psych.ucsc.edu/faculty/brogoff/index.php?Bio

INDEX

eBooks – at www.eBookstore.tandf.co.uk

A library at your fingertips!

eBooks are electronic versions of printed books. You can store them on your PC/laptop or browse them online.

They have advantages for anyone needing rapid access to a wide variety of published, copyright information.

eBooks can help your research by enabling you to bookmark chapters, annotate text and use instant searches to find specific words or phrases. Several eBook files would fit on even a small laptop or PDA.

NEW: Save money by eSubscribing: cheap, online access to any eBook for as long as you need it.

Annual subscription packages

We now offer special low-cost bulk subscriptions to packages of eBooks in certain subject areas. These are available to libraries or to individuals.

For more information please contact webmaster.ebooks@tandf.co.uk

We're continually developing the eBook concept, so keep up to date by visiting the website.

www.eBookstore.tandf.co.uk